S0-AWR-383

S.

Meditation

JOURNEY TO THE SELF

~~~~~~

by Ardis Whitman

SIMON AND SCHUSTER / NEW YORK

To the memory of my husband
Who taught me so much
About loving, enjoying
and growing

PUBLISHED BY SIMON AND SCHUSTER
A GULF+WESTERN COMPANY
ROCKEFELLER CENTER, 630 FIFTH AVENUE
NEW YORK, NEW YORK 10020

DESIGNED BY IRVING PERKINS
MANUFACTURED IN THE UNITED STATES OF AMERICA

1 2 3 4 5 6 7 8 9 10

LIBRARY OF CONGRESS CATALOGING IN PUBLICATION DATA

WHITMAN, EVELYN ARDIS, 1905–
    MEDITATION : JOURNEY TO THE SELF.
    1. MEDITATION.   2. INTROSPECTION.   I. TITLE.
BL627.W49   291.4'3   75–44316
ISBN 0–671–22211–2

The author wishes to thank the following for their kind permission to reprint from previously published works:

The American Journal of Psychiatry and Stanley R. Dean, M.D., for material from *The American Journal of Psychiatry*, Vol. 130, pp. 1036–1038, copyright 1973 The American Psychiatric Association; this material also appeared in *Psychiatry and Mysticism* by Stanley R. Dean, M.D., Chicago: Nelson-Hall Company, 1975.

Atheneum Publishers for material from *A Season in Heaven* by William Gibson, copyright © 1974 Tamarack Publications, Ltd.

The Christian Century Foundation for material from "Altered Consciousness: What the Research Points Toward," by Bill D. Schul, in the January 19, 1972, issue of *The Christian Century*, copyright 1972 Christian Century Foundation; and from "Going East: Neomysticism

Contents

~~~~~~

Preface / 11

1. *A Time of Need: A Time of Hope* / 17

2. *The Foothills of Discovery* / 31

3. *One Is All; All Is One* / 52

4. *The Quiet Revolution* / 70

5. *How Long Will It Last?* / 98

6. *Learning to Meditate* / 119

7. *The Joyful Rhythm* / 147

8. *The Tree of Tomorrow* / 166

What we have to be is what we are.

—The Asian Journal of Thomas Merton

Preface

~~~~~~

When I was a little girl, no doubt none too well-behaved, my parents, trying to practice the new "enlightened" theory that to spank a child was to thwart his growing personality, used to sit me in an austere, seldom-used parlor, there to "meditate" on how wrong it was to have stolen the neighbor's apples, or to have climbed to the top of the shed roof and jumped off, or to have thrown a chunk of firewood at my brother when he refused to surrender the swing.

I remember these crimes quite well, but have no recollection of the content of those half-hour "meditations" which followed them. But I'd be surprised if they strayed far from "I'm going to find out who told on me about the apples," "If I stay here any longer the other kids will go down to the river without me," "I hurt my foot when I jumped off the roof, so I guess I won't do it anymore— unless somebody dares me," or, at best, a hasty, insincere apology to my parents' deity—just in case, as I had been told, he really did watch everything that children were doing.

The only relationship these periods had to meditation was the existence of solitude. But there were other times when I came closer, wandering on a child's shore of self-discovery.

I was not, most of the time, a solitary child. Rather, I was a tomboy, a baseball player, a champion tree climber willing to walk a mile in order to show any challenger that no tree could daunt me. Nevertheless, I was no stranger to an inwardness vastly different from the parentally enforced meditation in the parlor; and there were times when true solitude mattered passionately—times when the six-pointed perfection of a snowflake described a world I sensed and longed to reach; times when the edge of the sea seemed the edge of eternity and I could watch the breaking waves endlessly, oblivious to the passing of time; times when, in cobwebbed haymows, dark and fragrant, sunlight coming in thin spears of radiance through dusty windows, I sought an inward journey not knowing it by name.

A January day comes back to me. I am skating and I am alone. Behind the island in the cove I have been whirling boastfully, making great convoluted figures on the ice. Suddenly there is a roar and a rumble and a train appears in the distance about to cross the bridge over the cove. It is twilight of the short winter day, and the windows of the train are already lighted. I rush toward it, electrified by the faces in the lighted windows. They are going, going. They will vanish around the turn under the trees and be gone forever, the laughing young couple, the old man with his face pressed against the window, the whole bright stream of passing life.

The train vanishes, though I long to hold it there frozen in time; and I skate away to the shore and sit on an overturned boat, letting this small stream of history go down, down—in a way I seemed always to have known how to do—into some other part of my mind where I understood better, cherished longer.

I remember still the sense of identity with the great bright train which rushed into the future with such explosive energy; but I remember as well a sense of kinship with the mysterious oncoming night around it—with the dark under the trees, with the first faint and distant stars, with that ringing sound that seems to fill the air on certain nights as though one hears the creaking of the universe.

Though I could not then find the words to say it—or even the clarity to make a wordless picture—I remember that I felt the energy of the train as though it were my own vitality and gregariousness rushing eagerly to the great cities of the world; to other human beings; to some joyful kind of work. But I felt also the mystery of sky and stars as a kind of hallowed milieu as real to my heart as the train and its people.

I don't think it occurred to me as a child to see these two worlds as the enemies of each other. For me, simply, it felt always as right and natural to take this inward journey, to grope for a wonderland in myself which I sensed but could not define, as to skate in the winter and swim in the summer.

It still does; but, for me as for most people, this joyful rhythm is lost much of the time in a maze of clocks and schedules, of earning, worrying, achieving; and in the last decades journalists like myself have had far more reason to report on sociology and politics than on what is happening to the spirit of man.

Now suddenly all that has changed. At the turn of the

seventies we became a nation turning inward on a long journey in search of its soul; and with a sense of home-coming and an extra whetting of journalistic curiosity, I have been exploring over the last two years the nature and direction of this unexpected revolution, this deep-rooted and promising change in the lives of all of us.

As we shall see, what is happening is sometimes as innocent and childlike as the dreams of a child on the edge of the sea; sometimes as fraudulent as a confidence man selling the Brooklyn Bridge; sometimes religious in the most profound and adult sense of the word; sometimes a sophisticated laboratory-centered effort to research an important and hitherto largely unexplored part of the human psyche.

As we shall also see, this journey inward is not always a gentle one; but then neither is any kind of learning; and, in the opinion of the scholars, scientists and mystics I've talked to in these transforming years, the struggle is worth it, for—they think—this is a learning whose time has come.

They may well be right. I find myself remembering suddenly an autumn day back in the mid-sixties when racial tensions were at their highest. That day I went into Harlem with a microphone and asked the people I met what hope they had, what they felt might come of all this in the end. Some had too much hate to answer a white person; some spoke of fear; a few hoped; but one quiet man, perhaps fifty, looked up from a newsstand's disaster headlines at which he had been staring blankly for a long time, and he said, "The trouble is we don't know what it is just to be people, just to be human. We don't know how to treat ourselves, and so we don't know how to treat each other."

In the end this book is about that—about what it is to

be human and hence to understand ourselves and each other; about closing the gap between inwardness and action; about using, at last, the whole of the human potential; about *becoming* what in fact we are.

CHAPTER 1

A Time of Need: A Time of Hope

〰〰〰〰〰〰〰〰〰〰〰〰〰〰〰〰〰〰〰〰〰〰〰〰〰〰

A change is happening to us in the seventies—a change that in the end may be more monumental than the alteration of our lives which came with the riots and storms of the tumultuous sixties. If it is a revolution—and I think it is—it makes no sound on the streets, it bombs no buildings, carries no placards, wields no weapons. But once you have begun to look, you find it everywhere—changing institutions, changing thinking, changing lives.

All of a sudden—or so it seems—people are turning inward, eagerly exploring the lost kingdoms of inner space. Centers of meditation blossom on college campuses; business concerns sponsor contemplative retreats; institutions for the mentally ill experiment with meditation as therapy; architects set up "contemplative environments."

As we shall see, the roots of this movement are deep in the past, even in the immediate, seemingly so different past; but to the casual eye it seems to have sprung up overnight. Who would have thought ten years ago that in the year 1975 Indian gurus and swamis would be in demand in science laboratories; that the American Psychiatric Association would officially study meditation and mysticism; that serious meditators in the United States would run into the millions?

What we are seeing appears like a strange forest grown from seeds that no one knew had been planted. But, however that may be, it is here and we must decide whether to nurture or destroy this new growth in our lives. We will not make sense of that decision until we find out where the new growth came from and what it can do for us; and it is these two questions that are, in the main, what this book is about.

Where, then, *did* it come from? Why have we leaped from the activist sixties to the meditating, inward seventies? Why is a nation which could supply the sophisticated hardware to go to the moon now sitting on cushions, contemplating mandalas?

It is probable that most Americans—if they could be induced to answer the question at all—would say, "It's the old pendulum effect. People are tired of what they were doing. They'd like a little rest and quiet." My husband, with his gift for clarity, said simply, "We're going inside because we're tired of the outside."

There is no doubt that that is true. We are tired to death of crises, disasters, and problems we can't solve; and cycles of inwardness *do* often come when nations are floundering and accustomed ways of life no longer seem to work. Overwhelmed, people *do* take refuge in a kind of isolationism, a saving of their own souls, a place within where no one can ask anything more of them.

The retreat is real. But many thoughtful commentators agree that it goes deeper than a mere self-concerned isolationism. They believe that it expresses *disillusionment*—

often a thought-through, concern-for-others disillusionment which is far more pertinent, and historically more
important, than a simple, selfish running away.

This disillusionment, moreover, has a special significance, for it is one of the many points at which the seemingly so different sixties and seventies come together and
show the strength of their linkage. No journalist traveling
and interviewing in the middle decades of the twentieth
century can fail to have encountered this disillusionment
again and again—sometimes in forms as unforgettable as
a branding iron.

I was in Stockholm in the late sixties when the flight of
American deserters and draft dodgers to Sweden first came
to public attention, and one day I met a blond boy from
a Midwest farm who tried to explain why he had fled the
Army and, with it, the home and country he loved. He
didn't talk much. He was not a very articulate person. He
simply showed me a drawing he had made. It was very de-
tailed and it had taken him a long time. It was a drawing
of an eye, a gigantic eye, magnified many times—and reflected in it was a chaos of exploding bombs, of dying,
burning children, leveled villages, dead forests, booby-
trapped roads with legless soldiers lying beside them.

That was in the sixties. But in Denver last year I asked
the young American vice-president of the Eastern faith,
Ananda Marga, why he had taken up this new belief. He
answered at once. "I was in Vietnam," he said earnestly.
"I wanted to know why I was there. We had been given
a set of values, and I began to see where those values had
led me and I felt there must be another way."

Another way, another way! In my memory, these two
words are like a drumbeat accompanying the journeyings
of both the sixties and the seventies, and they sound the

same in both decades. I hear them in hundreds of voices
—voices of the cities, the ghetto, the small town; voices
of the left-out; especially voices of the young; a chorus of
voices all saying in different ways one thing: "I *know* there
is a better way to live." Illustrations race through my
memory. I remember a young man ready to leave a good
job for a commune because, he insisted, "There's no way
that this way of life can be right for me." I remember a
taxi driver in Harlem who was asked if he was happy and
answered with a sweep of his arm out the window to the
streets around him, in one word—"Here?" And I remember a young man who stood next to me at the rear of an
auditorium where an enormous crowd of young people
waited for the arrival of another seer from the East. The
young man was a college graduate who had given up his
profession to follow after a strange and certainly prob-
lematic new religion. When I asked him why, he said
with passion, "We've seen that our parents with their
Cadillacs and their Florida vacations have precious little
to tell us about the way to peace and love."

The disillusionment these youngsters are talking about
is not theirs alone. It has been expressed in other ways by
their elders for a long time, until the words have grown
so axiomatic that we hardly notice them anymore. Our
times are "sterile," say the sophisticated voices of this disillusionment; "artificial," "inhuman," "materialistic."
Therefore, we are "alienated," we feel "powerless," "cut
off from our real selves," "unreal," "lonely." What it all
adds up to was expressed concisely by theologian Harvey
Cox in his book *The Feast of Fools.* "While gaining the
whole world," he said, Western man "has been losing his
own soul."

From my own reporting I can testify that thousands of

people do feel just that way. They feel that somehow they have been robbed, that a thing very precious to them has fallen through the interstices of the pipes and the wires and the computers of a technological, rational world and vanished.

Moreover, of late, disillusionment with the successes of a technological age—a disillusionment which already has shown a sufficient vitality to start us toward the discovery of new values—has been hastened by the contemporary realization that the technological age is failing even on its own terms. Our air is polluted; our planet can be blown up; there are too many weapons; people are starving; and, as the final blow, it turns out that we've used too much of our resources on wonderful new inventions and that there may not be enough to go around anymore.

In February of 1975, the magazine *U.S. News & World Report* ran a research piece called "How America Is Changing." It reported that church leaders and scholars found "widespread disillusionment with the material progress and big institutions that have preoccupied Americans since the end of World War I," that there was a "wide-ranging distrust of United States leadership and institutions." And it quoted a Harris poll which found that, with few exceptions, confidence in major institutions is down sharply from 1966—sometimes drastically—and that confidence in the executive branch of the U. S. government fell in that period from 41 percent to 19 percent, and confidence in major companies from 55 percent to 29 percent.

The unquestioned trust in the old order and its values has vanished—apparently for good—and with its vanishing there is a tremendous and natural sense of a need for rethinking. If we weren't right before, people reason, shouldn't we stop now and try to find out where we went wrong? Shouldn't we try to find out what a human being really is and what he can be?

"We need to take back inside ourselves the enormous amount of things that are happening outside," urges psychoanalyst James Hillman, director of studies at the C. G. Jung Institute in Zurich, Switzerland. Several years ago when psychiatrist Erich Fromm was asked, in the question period following a lecture, for a practical answer to the problems of living, he said promptly, "Quietness. Concentration for a half hour every day, twice a day if possible." And in the moment of disappointment that followed so simplistic an answer, he added, "You have to stop in order to be able to change directions." Still another commentator, the brilliant evolutionist Loren Eiseley, put it this way: "From a theoretical desire to *understand* the universe, we have come to a point where it is felt we *must* understand it to survive."

We must understand to survive. This is the conviction that has, in considerable part, triggered the inward revolution; a conviction felt alike by "ordinary" people far too inarticulate to express its full content and by people of intellectual stature who know consciously and exactly what they mean when they say it. What we have lost, they feel, is something we can find only in human beings themselves—in their sensitivity, their vision, their still undiscovered resources. So a vanguard of searching minds is turning inward on a voyage of exploration as courageous as the voyages which took the ancient mariners to the edges of their world and beyond into unknown space.

Already messengers are coming back from these new Spice Islands, this new Cathay, with remarkable tales. Maps—still primitive, but maps nonetheless—are being drawn; produce is returning in the holds of the ships. In fact, whether coincidentally or by cause and effect, our time of great need appears in conjunction with a time of overwhelming discovery about the nature of the mind, about its wonders and its possibilities.

Or, to put it another way, at the same time that people are despairing of the tarnished model of man, ways of changing the model are appearing everywhere. In fact, the title of this chapter is intentionally twofold. We have embarked on this voyage because our need is so great; but also because we're beginning to discover something about the treasure which waits for us. Everywhere there are signs of a coming era of extended mental abilities. We are, moreover, in the midst of an exploring age. In search of treasure and discovery, we go down to the floor of the sea, scale the highest mountains, even journey toward the stars. With the same intent, we go to the depths of our own consciousness, lured there by travelers' tales of wonder.

They come from every direction, these promises. With some hesitation one must include—indeed, one must begin with—the drug culture. Though damaging in many ways, the drug culture introduced a hidden world in human beings, announced as well that this hidden world is available to everyone, and insisted that the urge to alter consciousness is a natural and proper one.

"I was in college, in business administration, planning to go in with my father," one young man told me. "All of a sudden I was turned on to marijuana and LSD. It opened up another idea of what the mind is. I found that I was running after authors and teachers to see what they said of love and life." He is now president of Ananda Marga in the United States and has long since given up drugs, but they were a trigger. Psychedelic research has shown, says research psychiatrist Stanislav Grof, "that the mystical and religious experiences are primary phenomena intrinsic to human nature."

Promise and discovery come also from the mobility of our generation: the constant intermingling of the traveling young of all nations; the continuous exchanging of ideas; the sensing—sometimes subliminal sensing—of other patterns of life; and, specifically, the infiltration of the Eastern faiths into the Western world.

It misses the point, I think, for churchmen to object, as some do, to the rapid infiltration of Eastern theology into the Western world. The service the Eastern faiths have performed for us does not consist in bringing us a new theology; nor is such a theology likely to be taken up by many Americans. Rather, they bring us a rebirth of belief in the validity and importance of the inner self, the spiritual psyche. Of course, meditation, mysticism, stress on inwardness, needn't have waited on the arrival of cults from the East. Traditionally, these things are a part of church and synagogue. Many of the great holydays of Judaism have been set up, wrote Rabbi Joshua Liebman in *Peace of Mind*, to "serve as vehicles for the encouragement of self-communion and confession." And the Christian faith is founded not only on love of one's fellow man but on the conviction that the kingdom of heaven is within. But in the age of the secular city, Western faiths have drifted away from that heritage; and the entry of the East into our lives is helping to restore the balance.

Altogether, what we are discovering is that we are simply more than we have thought ourselves to be. We are finding to our astonishment that we have more "mind" than we thought we had, more ways of thinking and knowing and being than we had imagined. Our despair and disillusion have contributed to that discovery; so has our mobility; so has our experience of the world of psychedelic drugs and our experience of the mystic wisdom of the Eastern faiths.

But perhaps the most astonishing contribution has come from the science laboratory. Reluctantly at first, but now in considerable numbers, scientists are lending their support to the quiet revolution. Is it true that a yogi can lie on a bed of nails without injury? Somewhere, you may be sure, some scientist is trying to find out. Is it true that meditation can increase one's health and energy and bring relaxation and peace of mind? Whether it is true or not, the exploration is no longer being left solely to monks and gurus.

In fact, it may well be that no historical change has had a greater effect in turning us inward than the new exploration in the laboratories. The laboratory, pummeled like church, government and school for its failure to give us a livable human world, has left its pulpit of certainties and, along with many of the rest of us, is deep in journeys to the inner world and states of altered consciousness. In fact, even before the coming of the revolutions of the sixties and the seventies, natural scientists were dealing in the mysterious and the incomprehensible. Bandying around unscientific-sounding words and phrases like "quarks" and "black holes in space," they came up with pronouncements fully as hard to believe as are auras and angels and turned to areas of research which partner the new revolution. Neurologists began to study the brain, revealing marvels that dwarf our greatest technological achievements; astronomers revealed a universe stretching in magnitude and majesty far beyond the greatest imaginings of even a generation ago; physicists have abandoned cause and effect for a universe much stranger than the world of *Alice in Wonderland.*

As for behavioral scientists, it is impossible to chronicle in the space of this book what is happening in the laboratories across the country. In the not so distant past, everything relating to the psychic was anathema to psychologists and psychiatrists. "Who would have thought ten years ago," says Dr. Stanley Dean, who moderated an historic panel on meditation and related topics at a recent American Psychiatric Association meeting, "that medical science would be interested in meditation?" Equally, who would have thought the behavioral sciences would explore mysticism and listen with respect to psychic healers? Since the early years of the century when William James studied altered states of consciousness, behavioral scientists have almost entirely repudiated the fields of extrasensory perception and mysticism. But now, as we shall see, research in these areas and in the control of mind over body is going on in literally hundreds of universities and laboratories in a sudden explosion of knowledge and discovery. Even a preliminary look turns up a tremendous range of experiments: experiments in psychokinetics; in the ability of trained meditators to increase production of alpha and theta brain waves; in dream as a preview of the future; in the likelihood that energy waves are emitted into the atmosphere by all forms of life; in the relationship of human beings to geophysical rhythms; and so forth.

The result is an impressive scientific documentation which gives respectability to the inward journey, a respectability which has been lost for a long, long time. Dr Barbara Brown, a talented researcher in biofeedback, who has worked for eleven years in the laboratories of the Veterans Administration Hospital in Sepulveda, California, under limited grants from the National Institute of Mental Health, says emphatically, "The explosion of interest in the magic of the mind is not an emotional reaction of a perplexed society; it results from objective confirmation that the mind, the psyche, the soul, the emotion of man possess powerful abilities and energies."

Moreover, these discoveries are not only accumulating but spiraling—one might almost say heavenward! Beginning with a pragmatic search for new techniques, they are being steadily pushed by the evidence in the direction of a once unthinkable position—the acceptance of something like a spirit, a soul in man. Dr. Elmer Green at the prestigious Menninger Institute in Topeka, Kansas, is quoted as saying:

> We are learning a great deal about the human mind, how it functions, how it learns, and this, in time, should have quite an impact on the whole educational process. But perhaps of even greater importance, science is beginning to confirm many of our religious and mystical traditions. In the past science has been criticized as the antithesis of religion, but today a body of evidence is growing which indicates that the higher levels of consciousness are not only a reality but also a legitimate business of science.

Depth psychology, in fact, has taken over some of the emphasis of religion. "The unconscious is the door through which we pass to find the soul," says psychoanalyst Hillman in his book *Insearch*. And he adds, "As the churches emptied, the clinics filled and the depth psychologists—especially Jung—seemed to find soul and a living God-image in the midst of their work."

Scientists who agree with such ideas are beginning to

organize and join forces with agreeing people from other disciplines. For example, a group of educators, psychiatrists and psychologists, mathematicians, physicists and theologians met in 1971 in Council Grove, Kansas, to set up an international conference, the Inter-disciplinary Conference on the Voluntary Control of Internal States of Consciousness, and announced a shared belief that man is not only a physical, mental and emotional being but also a spiritual being. There is also a new and very active branch of psychology, Transpersonal, that openly and frankly concerns itself with higher states of consciousness and with the spiritual search which it asserts is an essential aspect of human life.

In fact, now that we look back with hindsight, we can see that the behavioral sciences—and, since Einstein, the natural ones as well—have been almost inevitably leading in this direction. The more they study, the more the physicists discover a world of mystery which man's utmost ingenuity cannot unravel; and the behavioral scientists have contributed over a long period of time simply by stressing the existence of a buried self, the unconscious. Many commentators have pointed out that psychoanalysis has unwittingly helped to prepare people for the turn to inwardness by making it easier to imagine depth upon depth in the mind, depths normally dormant until their powers of energy are released. Ira Progoff, who wrote the important book *The Death and Rebirth of Psychology*, says elsewhere that "while depth psychology began with a materialist, psychiatric orientation, the experience of its most creative researchers turned it in the opposite direction, moving toward the creative and spiritual potential of human nature."

The relationship of these new and exciting developments to the expanding consciousness that characterizes the inward revolution is multiple and obvious; and it would be remarkable indeed if our lives were not changed by it. Once shaken, the old hitherto inviolable concepts of cause and effect can never be quite the same again; nor can rationalism hold an undisputed sway. The essence of the change is that people who have a natural longing for the inward path find the journey mapped and permission given. The way in is available; the experiences are available.

But scientific support, though of tremendous importance, is only one of the many yeasty new developments which are springing us from our long imprisonment in a narrow region of ourselves. "Where is all the interest coming from?" I asked a bearded young friend who, with his wife and new baby, live by choice on a Maine island, eating a macrobiotic diet and spending much time in meditation. "From astrology," he said, "and sociology, and psychiatry, and new ways of loving each other. It's like a wind. It comes from everywhere and everything."

Summing up, the influences that have shaped this tremendous change seem to be twofold—despair and hope, a matrix that has had great evolutionary power at crises of civilization in the past. And as this contrapuntal movement continues its cumulative effect it produces a third and perhaps the most important reason for the coming of the new age—the discovery among steadily growing numbers of people of the rewards of meditation and, indeed, the rewards of the whole inward movement.

A new chapter in our history is being written, and it is time for believers and skeptics alike to understand not only why it is happening but what is involved. How do people find their way inward? And what do they discover there? What are the personal experiences of the people who meditate? The individual people—the boy or girl in the commune, the experimenter in the laboratory, the Quaker in the pew, the monk in his cell, the contemplative in the Arizona desert? And how can these experiences help us live responsibly in our turbulent troubled world?

CHAPTER 2

The Foothills of Discovery

〜〜〜〜〜〜〜〜〜〜〜〜〜〜〜〜〜〜〜〜〜〜〜〜〜

It is not easy to define meditation. Here and there across the country this past year, I have asked people how *they* would define this new-old skill. Some simply didn't know. Others were involved in it and came up with reasonably sophisticated answers. Still others confidently offered what seemed to be the views of average Americans.

"I meditate a lot," one man told me; "I often sit down and figure out what to do about my problems." "Meditation is sort of being quiet. It's like daydreaming," hazarded another. "It's kind of talking to yourself," an elderly woman who lives alone said with a sigh.

As we shall see, these definitions are wide of the mark. They are like a child's-eye view of the life of a great university. Nevertheless, they are understandable; for the truth is that meditation, like everything of importance, is complex and many-layered. It is difficult to define, in the first place, because we need a language for it. The words that we have to describe the inward, the psychic happenings that have become so important to so many people in this last third of a traumatic century sound odd and esoteric to the inexperienced who are thus diverted from understanding and using a very normal human activity.

Meditation is also difficult to define because it covers so wide a range. The word has been used to describe a whole series of inner happenings from the most peaceful to the most turbulent, a whole series of approaches from the intense discipline of the monk in his cell to the easy, restful "twenty minutes morning and night" of Transcendental Meditation.

The map of meditation, in short, is as wide as the soul of man, stretching from the worker at his bench to the monk in his cell, from the little territory of everyday problems to the mountain summit where men search for God. And the joys and discoveries of meditation cover a range from brilliant, unforgettable imagery on the screen of the mind to the sublime "nothingness" of the lifelong contemplative; from the sick man's discovery that there is in himself a sanctuary from his pain to the peak experience of the meditator caught in an awareness of the world around him; from the "peace of mind" of the layman who has learned to turn off the world for a few minutes to the hard-won wisdom of artist and statesman.

What can such extremes have in common? What do devoted disciplined monks and nuns share with a horde of young people chanting mantras at the feet of their favorite guru? What do the scholarly, profound people in Zen Buddhist study centers have in common with pragmatic psychologists testing biofeedback and altered consciousness in the laboratory?

What, in short, *is* meditation? Perhaps before we try to answer that we must first say what it is *not*. It is certainly not what was happening to me, a small girl sitting rebelliously in my mother's parlor; nor would it have been even had my sins weighed a little more heavily and been perceived more clearly. Meditation is not simply "thinking about," whether the thinking is about one's sins or one's virtues, about the perfection of a sunset, or even about the meaning of God. The meditator is not a person who sits struggling over his problems; and meditation is not a hashing or rehashing of one's past mistakes, a conscious effort to resolve by mental wrestling the dilemmas of one's life.

True, the dictionary defines it in part as "serious and substantial reflection"; but such a definition has little or nothing to do with what millions of meditators practice, and still less to do with the classic traditions.

In fact, there is a sense in which meditation is antithetical to the conscious mind. In a long, tape-recorded conversation, Dr. Robert Masters, whose sophisticated experiments we will encounter later in the book, told me that meditation "is always an altered state of consciousness, always a departure from the normal experience of the person no matter what kind of meditation it is." Most qualified teachers of the art would agree. Meditation, they would say, is a way of *relinquishing* the hold of everyday styles of thinking, a way of going down to reaches of the mind deeper than those that we normally use.

It leads, in fact, beyond ordinary consciousness to other levels of being; to that place in the self where, it is hoped, knowledge, wisdom, enlightenment and joy will be found. To understand what that means one needs to recall what human beings have always known about the nature of their minds. Most of us are not very articulate about it, yet no one really has much trouble understanding that we *do* have another, larger self. Long before anyone had ever heard the word "unconscious," human beings knew that there was an everyday mind and another mind—that there was a place in the self where you dealt with cooking the meat for dinner and manipulating stocks on the market, and another place in the self where you could, if you would, be "real."

After all, from the beginning of time people have experienced states of consciousness that they realize are different from their ordinary waking state. Sleep and dream, of course; but also "peak experience"; sudden inexplicable bursts of creativity; daydreaming so profound that it feels close to trance; the ecstasy of love; the rapturous sense of being close to all that lives.

From the beginning of time people have also been aware, however dimly, that these intimations, these signals, these passing winds of knowledge, spring from within themselves; from another self somehow resident under the persona of everyday. Who has not felt the mysterious edge of this "other": the feeling on some spring night, some winter dawn, that there is a unity between ourselves and the cosmos, a link we could make but don't; that there is something ungrasped, something we almost reach, something that eludes us like a dream we are trying to remember when we wake? Emerson called it "the bright stranger, the foreign self."

We acknowledge this deep self, this other self, again and again. The language abounds with the phrases we use for it and every great visionary has found his own way of expressing it. The poet Dante called it "the natural fire within the dark wood of life"; and Job, "the place of understanding." There is a treasure hidden in the field, preached Jesus; and he said, "The kingdom of heaven is within you." It has been described as "the ground of the soul," "the inward voice," "the inner light," "the autonomous self," "the hidden life within the human psyche," and in many other ways.

"Ordinary" people also have words for it, words we often use casually, scarcely noticing that we do so. We say, "No one knows what I really feel deep down inside"; or "It wasn't the real me who did that"; or "I know it in my heart, but I can't say it." So, though it is only a metaphor to speak of "depth in myself," still the layered consciousness into which one goes deeper and deeper appeals to something real for all of us.

Meditation, then, is a way of access to this deep self, and its range is so great because the territory it leads to is so immense and the capacity of human beings to enter and enjoy that territory differs so widely. Meditation is as diversified as human beings themselves, and, moreover, it is a journey of spiraling joy. In fact, the art of meditation is much like going up a mountain. Even in the foothills, the air is fresher than it was when you started your climb, and the view is wider; but the higher you go the more there is to see, the more beauty there is to enjoy, the more experience and wisdom there are to bring back.

Yet, though one senses progression, one names the steps of this staircase reluctantly; for who can assess one man's joy against another's sense of All in Nothing? One man's insight against another's peace of mind?

Reluctantly, too, because, in speaking of the journey to the self one is even more apt to speak of depth than height. The meditator speaks alternately—and apparently interchangeably—of rising, growing, reaching, climbing, and of going down, down into the depths of himself. A paradox; and the interchange must be accepted without complaint, for, in fact, in the domain of the meditator, height and depth mysteriously are one, and the metaphors do not alter the fact that in meditation there is beginning and there is growing, there is light on practical problems and there is the experience of satori, there is healing of the body and there is illumination of the mind.

I remember a man worried by an emotionally disturbed wife and a drug-addicted teen-age son, who told me that when things were at their worst he'd go out in his sailboat. Then, he said, "I don't think about my troubles. I concentrate on the sun on the water; I watch the sails bending in the wind. Sometimes I meditate. I seem to move into a quiet place somewhere, where I am just myself—not myself plus my problems. If I think at all I think about all the other men who have put out to sea behind sails like these, and I wonder what they thought about and where they went and what they saw. By the time I'm inbound, my mind is calm and I can go back to what is troubling me. Then sometimes I imagine that a friend of mine is sailing with me, that these are his troubles and not mine, and that I'm trying to give him a hand. That way I stop going round and round in my own private little hell and begin to see things as they are."

This is certainly the kindergarten of meditation, but even here some basic requirements have been met. My sailboat friend had chosen a quiet place, left behind the frantic millrace of daily life, and, with what little knowledge he had, *tried* to go down below the surface of life, not only to the knowledge of self but to the source of self. For a while, he had said, "I think of nothing at all." A beautiful phrase to describe all meditation—whether it is a temporary quietness to prepare for the solving of dilemmas or the disciplined entry into peace and "nothingness" of the seekers for satori—is the long-used Quaker phrase "centering down." In such a context meditation can be, even at its simplest, not a conscious wrestling with problems but a prelude to insight about them, a "going down" into a place of greater wisdom.

As noted earlier, "to think about" is not in itself meditation—though in the West it is more likely to have that connotation than in the East. But if we have shut out the disturbing, competitive world, "turned off" the jangling of our own egos—our ambitions, our injured pride, our fears—and centered down into the sanctuary of our deepest selves, we may find ourselves emerging with a new understanding of the problems of our lives, an enlightenment about some person, some situation, some dream, some hazard, important to us.

More important, if we have grown used to meditating without conscious purpose over a period of time, if we know "the way down," we not only gain insight on our daily problems but *train ourselves* to be the kind of people who find solutions, who teach themselves to go to the heart of whatever troubles them. Moreover, such meditation keeps us from losing our flexibility, our sensitiveness, our power of growth. It may be the very beginning of meditation's rewards, but it is not small or unimportant; and it has suddenly taken on a new significance, for to survive today in the confusion of a changing world we must all become problem-solvers, facing new demands with new talents, new strengths and new solutions.

A more significant form of meditation is the attempt at understanding what manner of person it is who is doing this searching. Meditation can be *a very intense form of self-examination:* Who am I? What is being asked of me? Why am I here? What do I really want? These are the classic questions which have plagued mankind since the beginning of time.

Who does not want to "find" himself, be himself? We are all masked, we are all behind bars, locked in prisons we have made for ourselves. Most of us are consciously aware that we make a very narrow use of our gifts—that we are masked not only from the rest of the world but from our own scrutiny, unable to understand who we are or to be what we are sure we could be. We know a great deal about how to do things, but not much about what ought to be done and why; and we feel much of the time in our adult life that we are imitations of ourselves. "I am not myself," we say when we have done something that displeases us, or when we feel vague, disconnected from life, unable to communicate. But what is "myself"?

No frantic mental running about, denouncing, excusing, dividing one's self, will help to answer that question. It must begin with a quieting of the waters so that we can see below the stormy surface.

One day at a center for contemplation in the Arizona desert, I followed a girl who went about playing a guitar. I knew who she was: not a resident but a guest like myself, she had come from the city—where she had a nondescript office job—seeking something, as I was. On her way back from her solitary wandering one day, she saw me and sat down beside me.

"What are you looking for here?" I asked her.

"Myself," she said without hesitation. "In the city at my job I am, like everyone else, just somebody who does things. But I know I am more than that. I want to explore myself, be myself more fully."

The wish can be a self-centered egotistic one; but for her—as for many others—it had a nobler context: the belief that, as psychiatrist Rollo May once wrote, man's consciousness of himself is the source of his highest qualities. "The more self-awareness a person has," he said, "the more alive he is." And there is a Zen saying, "If you wish to seek the Buddha, you ought to see into your own nature." Indeed, Zen was originally called "seeing into one's own nature."

But what is "myself"? And where shall we go to find it? The epigraph at the front of this book is Thomas Merton's "What we have to be is what we are." It is a beautiful but mysterious phrase. How do we know what we are so that we can be it? I remember a drunk who attached himself to me on a train one time, repeating over and over again, "What's it all about? Do you know? What's it all about? Why don't I know who I am? Do you know who I am?"

One's lifetime is a constant search for the answer to that question. That meditation aids such discovery is beautifully illustrated in a story from the laboratories at Menninger, where experienced meditators have, from time to time, been tested against control groups. During meditation, a thirty-year-old physicist with whom Dr. Green and his wife—also a psychiatrist—had discussed occult metaphysics "became aware," say the Greens,

> of being in a long gray tunnel at the end of which was a bright light. With great joy he realized that this light was his life's goal and began running toward it. As he neared the light, however, its brilliance began to hurt him and he saw that the light came from an intensely illuminated figure of himself which was upside-down, balanced head-to-head on top of another figure of himself. The lower figure was non-illuminated and his normal self and he wanted to run up and merge with the illuminated man. The pain of the brilliance became so terrifying, however, that he was forced to flee back down the tunnel.

At this point, say the Greens, "the experience ended and he began an examination of his inner nature."

Such discovery often emerges from the habitual practice of meditation, for maturity and self-understanding are among its rewards. In time spent with the inner self we see, often in symbolic but meaningful language, how we make the same mistakes over and over; we see how painfully we dilute our ability to love by vanity and bitterness and sloth; we see in how many ways we grow older without growing wiser. We see what we long to be and how far it is from where we are.

Surprisingly, we also *discover our bodies.* Far from trying to forget the existence of the body, skilled meditators give it respectful attention, both because of the power it has to divert the seeking and because of the mystique of the alliance of body and spirit. Of course, the Eastern mystics have always understood the tremendous link between knowledge of the body and knowledge of the self and of the gods. Westerners, conditioned both by Plato's views and by Saint Paul's, see body and spirit as separate and even alien to each other, and often maintain the most distant acquaintance with the complaints and resources of that wonderful instrument, our physical selves.

For children, even Western children, body and self are one. But somehow over the years mind and body divide, trip over each other, imprison each other, and our bodies become strangers to us; even the realization of their "wellness" or illness is hidden from us. How odd it is that most of the time we live our lives as strangers to our own physical selves! "It is surprising how many people have only a general acquaintance with what they feel . . .," writes Rollo May. "They tell you they feel fine, or lousy, as vaguely as though they were saying 'China is in the Orient.' Their connection with their feelings is as removed as if over a long-distance telephone."

So it is one of the great joys of contemporary training in meditation that—in group experiences at least—so much time is given to the re-experiencing of the body. I am thinking about a summer morning a couple of years ago when a group of us were invited backstage at the New York Ballet theater in Saratoga Springs for some experiments in sensitivity with a visiting group. Among other things, we were asked to stand, two by two, a multitude of strangers, a little timid, staring curiously at each other, and surrounded by a circle of watchers too afraid to try whatever unknown experiment was coming. Then we were instructed to watch each other's body language and try to copy it. My partner was a teacher of dance, and I was painfully aware of my awkward efforts to copy the grace-ful movement of her hands flung up like birds coasting on the wind, her body supple as a convoluting vine. But all day I found myself thinking in ways I had not thought before, aware of myself as a muted voice with a language yet to learn.

Yoga exercises and dance are often used in conjunction with meditation, especially the dance called Tai-Chi—the flowing ancient movements used two thousand years before Christ, movements which supposedly are in accordance with nature's flow; and in sensitivity and encounter groups people are often instructed to touch each other. Nothing is easier to ridicule than the clutchings and gropings which often ensue. But, at the root, something of importance is happening. For example, at a recent Esalen conference we were instructed to take partners and, eyes closed, explore each other's hands and then faces, searching for new understanding of bone structure, temperature, texture, meditating as we did so. I felt awkward and uncomfortable, and alien too to my partner, whose hands seemed soft and chilly and whose temperament appeared aggressive. But then we were instructed to take our part- ners' faces in our hands. Her face was warm. Her very life seemed to be cupped under her chin, cupped in my hand— a life timid, appealing, a surprise.

The body, understood, taken down with us into the deep self, has lessons to teach and lessons to learn. It helps to have instructions in these lessons; but even the average person, sitting alone in quiet contemplation, can get a new sharpened sense of the miracle of his physical being by such artless devices as taking note of the movement of the wind across his face, feeling muscles move and flex at his behest, trying new ways of breathing.

Many practitioners, in fact, believe that all problems and all aspects of character and personality show up in the body, and that learning to understand the body's signals can wake to aliveness both body and mind. In fact, in a real sense what is going on here is a revaluing of the hu- man body—a revaluing and hence an understanding of its linkage with mind, spirit, and with all living things.

In time and with practice, the linkage matters to you very much indeed. A few months ago, and for the first time in a very healthy life, I was suddenly stricken with what appeared to be an extremely serious illness. The doc- tors took a grim view, and I was sent to the hospital for several weeks, to undergo a long and painful series of tests. One night, before the worst of them, the nurse came in as usual with a sleeping pill. I had thought I would want it very much. Who would wish to endure wakefulness in the long hours of such an anxious night? But accustomed as I was by that time to "centering down," to going to an in- ward place for strength and knowledge, I now found that there was something I wanted to learn even more than I wanted sleep. At this moment, with awareness so heightened, I wanted to think through the relationship of body and spirit, of mysterious cells and blood and bone and heart; to the real Self so dependent on the body yet so separate from it. How did the "I" of bone and cell and corpuscle—this "I" which for the moment was in such trouble—relate to that real Self? And would that Self have any final influence, anything to say about the fragile envelope in which it was enclosed?

So I lay awake through the night, not brooding or worrying or praying, simply being aware of this congeries of myself, experiencing linkage and dimensions that had never been real to me before. It was a learning experience of great magnitude; and though it turned out that the disease I had been struck with was acute and it has healed and passed into oblivion, the depth of understanding that accompanied the apparent closeness of death will never be forgotten.

Meditation has a hundred ways to show us that body and spirit are one, to insure this closing of ranks among our divided selves. Experiments have shown that meditative periods can be like a fourth major state of consciousness. While we are meditating, our bodies are different; our minds are different; they relate to each other differently. "Neither waking, sleeping nor dreaming," writes John White, former director of education at the Institute of Noetic Sciences in Palo Alto, California, "the meditation state has been described as a 'wakeful hypometabolic condition.' Brain waves, heartbeat, blood pressure, breathing, galvanic skin resistance and many other factors are altered in meditation. Bodily functions slow to the point achieved in deep sleep and sometimes beyond, yet the meditator remains awake and emerges from meditation with a feeling of rest and loss of stress and tension."

Meditation is important to our knowledge of our identity as physical beings; but with the understanding of our bodies we only begin the answer to the perpetual question "Who am I?" Meditation is also a *journey through the mind itself.*

The mind, with its intricate processes, has always been a puzzle, mysterious as space, fascinating as the universe itself. We don't even understand the physiology of our brain, that part of the mind which we can probe and examine, that handful of pinkish-gray jelly which by some necromancy puts together ten watts of electricity and some chemicals and produces a theory of relativity and a Shakespearean sonnet, as well as every man's thoughts and opinions, hopes and skills. Psychologists and physiologists, probing, measuring, analyzing, have as yet few answers, but the further they go the more certain they are that we use only a small fraction of our mental capacities. We don't seem to know *how* to use more, and we are obstructed by the traditional education which tells us almost nothing about the marvelous instrument with which we learn.

In a very direct and experimental way meditators learn a great deal about how the mind works, just as the long-distance runner learns the power and flexibility of the body. Meditation is particularly valuable in helping us decipher the great puzzle of creativity. Where do these flashes of gigantic insight come from? How is the "Moonlight Sonata" born in the mind of Beethoven? How does the *Pietà* spring from the hands of Michelangelo?

Creative people have long known that deep reverie—shutting out the world and descending into the silence of one's self—can help produce music, art, writing, drama and the intuitions of scientists. Literature is full of stories of the trances from which artists emerge to write poems, compose symphonies, paint pictures, and scientists to announce a sudden image of truth. One thinks of Coleridge's "Kubla Khan"; of Handel's almost instantaneous pouring out of *Messiah*; of Archimedes' wild cry of "Eureka!" when, musing in his bathtub, he suddenly perceived the law of displacement.

Such events are part of the life story of almost all major artists and scientists; and of course no amount of meditation will turn the average person into a Beethoven or an Archimedes. But meditation can teach people to be far more creative than they have been in the past. "One has only to try the experiment of looking deeply within himself, . . . trailing almost any random idea," wrote Dr. May, "and he will find, so rich is a moment of consciousness in the human mind, that associations and new ideas beckon in every direction."

I remember a ride by the sea in Nova Scotia one summer day. I had chosen to sit with my niece's small daughter, six years old and much intrigued with her world. We were playing with numbers—"How many people in that car? How many American cars will we see? How many gulls on the roof of the fish house?" Suddenly she fell silent, preoccupied. We drove on by the sea with all its fascinating boats, past her favorite candy shop, and still she remained in some far-off place of her own. She did not hear what I was saying, so I was silent, too. Then she looked up from wherever she had been, eyes bright with discovery. "Numbers have no ending, do they?" she said in wonderment.

The tools for such discovery are in all of us; and, as we shall see, experimenters in contemporary laboratories often find startling proof of their existence in average people. Frequently people come to their first understanding of the extent of their own creativity through contemporary experiments in producing imagery by deep meditation or trance. A composer may emerge from such a trance with a melody ready to transcribe; a writer, ready to clear the problem of a chapter which has stalled him; and people of all kinds, with a memory of experiencing the structure and contour of their bodies, of looking at enchanted forests and luminous, brilliant colors they have never seen before, of "hearing" a flower, "seeing" a sound, discovering the marvel of light.

Through such experiences, the mind is jolted out of its old familiar tracks. In fact, meditation, far from being a way of escape, is a way to break from limited, logical categories of thought. Like Alice, we plunge through the looking glass into a world where reasons are turned upside down and values are different, and we return refreshed with new and vivid ideas of who we are and what life can be like.

Meditation has another way of helping us to know ourselves. It gives us a "great ease of access to lost memories." How much greater our experience is than the little span of our conscious knowledge! What we have felt and imagined, what we have dreamed and endured, what has influenced us and changed us—it's all there in our minds, but seemingly lost to us. The meditator, however, has a key to the subterranean vault where the past lives. At the simplest level meditators report hearing again the music of childhood, tasting the strawberry tarts, playing in the treetops of childhood orchards.

Last summer I had such an experience. I sat on the shore of the usually violent Bay of Fundy in Nova Scotia, on a limpid, lovely early evening, with a sea which defined the word "opalescent"—a sea so gentle that you could just

hear the sound of the tide against the rocks, air so clear
that the New Brunswick shore, forty miles away, seemed
to be within rowing distance.

I sat on a driftwood log (Where did it come from? The
wreckage of some ship? And before that a forest old and
distant?) and was aware for a while of nothing but the
monotone of the breaking waves. Gradually, out of a
memory which, to escape pain, had been buried more
deeply than the stones the sea had thrown up at my feet,
the faces of the past came back with the utmost clarity. I
saw my mother sitting on a great rock by another shore in
my childhood, her busy life suspended while she watched
the surf roll in against the pilings of a wharf I had not seen
in half a lifetime. I remembered—a memory I had not
thought of for a long time—paddling a canoe with my
brother in swift salty waters where, poor swimmers that
we were, we had no business to be; I "saw" a teen-age pic-
nic on this very shore on a moonlit evening with a great
fire of driftwood blazing in a cradle of the rocks.

Much of what we don't know is, in fact, in the tremendous storehouse of our memories. But we forget what
is stored there and thus lose it; or we persistently labor to
erase or distort our memories in order to give ourselves a
"better" self-image, or in order to rid ourselves of the
recollection of pain or the memory of joys which have
become too poignant in contrast to the present.

But it is not the memory itself but the understanding
which springs from it that is so valid and learning an experience. Meditation brings us back the thread of our
lives, their continuity, and we see our experiences not as
isolated events—now this happened, now that—but as a
flowing river carrying the awareness of who I was and who
I am. "Memories, good and bad, float to the top like

cream in coffee," an elderly meditator explained to me. "In the end what is really there is the sense of your life."

Sometimes, too, there is the sense of the journey of *all* life, beyond the circle of our own personal memories and experiences. Memories induced by meditation can be archetypal or simply historical—bringing back the knowledge that all men are one, that we share in a profound psychic sense the ancestral memory of human beings and not just of our lives.

I think of an hour last spring in the oak-shaded cemetery of a fourteenth-century church in Rye, England, beside the illegible headstones of the graves of my ancestors; and of an evening talking with an aging hero of the Resistance on a headland above the harbor in Oslo, Norway. On the very spot where the hostages of World War II were put to death, he told me their stories. I sat alone there when he had gone, and, in the darkness with the lights of ships so small and frail on the shadowed sea, I found myself aware of the thread of man's bravery, like a knotted skein leading out of a labyrinth.

These moments of meditation give us continuity. But paradoxically also they give us the knowledge of our own individuality, our separateness, and of the way we have spent our lives changing, changing. We try to blind ourselves to change—change in our situations, in the people around us, change in our ideas and perceptions; and we do this so that we will not have to change our actions. But in meditation the blindness falls away and it becomes clear that though the past is embodied in the present as the seed in the tree, seed and tree are different nonetheless; and change goes on ceaselessly, ceaselessly, this branch dying, that one coming to life.

Through meditation, then, we find our way to much knowledge about ourselves; but also, unexpectedly, meditating we *find each other*. One of the unexpected rewards of meditation, this most solitary of occupations, is that it is so communal, so instructive in the *art of love*.

A friend of mine once found herself on a beach at twilight. It was a time of grief for her, and she wanted very much to be by herself. But, it turned out, she was not quite alone. Offshore, across the darkening sea, was a single low island. Presently she was aware of a dim light moving on the island, and there came the splash of oars and the scrape of a boat leaving the shore. She made out the outlines of a fishing boat, and in it the figure of a man. He rowed a little way and anchored. My friend told me that after a while she felt an intense and glowing sense of oneness with that silent figure. It was as though sky and sea and night and those two solitary human beings were united in a kind of profound identity. "I was overtaken by joy," she said.

One of the best illustrations of this unity is that which comes when we have gone to the inner self in the way of those who have just lost someone much loved and who find that deep within at last they "understand" the lost one. Absorbed in their grief, they have shut out the jangling world and ceased for a while to care about getting ahead, making money, looking for pleasure. Like a mandala, the missing person is always before them, and their grief takes them into an inward journey where the one who is gone seems more clear, more understandable than when alive.

We understand the other person because we are there in the moment with them; but we also understand because when we go down into ourselves we leave behind the pettiness which so absorbs us. There is no room in this place, spacious though it is, for meanness, for the hate, the jealousy, the fear which cut us off from others. "It is not the desert island nor the stony wilderness that cuts you off from the people you love," wrote Anne Morrow Lindbergh in *Gift from the Sea*. "It is the wilderness in the mind, the desert in the heart through which one wanders, lost and a stranger." To put it simply, when I know myself, I know you too. In that serene and quiet place where I am learning about myself I realize that you too, like me, live in a world of tears, a world of failure; and, shut away in my own heart from competition with you, from the fears which divide us, I can see you with tenderness, knowing that we are one. Indeed, we are like torches lit from each other. Illumine the one and the other takes fire. As New York psychiatrist Jan Ehrenwald once told me, "The deeper we go, the closer we are."

It is *this* knowledge which accounts for the current popularity of meditating in groups, experiencing love and understanding in groups. "We flowed like a river; we were one," wrote a friend of a long-ago civil-rights march in Washington. And at a Quaker meetinghouse in New England, one participant, a somewhat austere history professor, rose at the end of a quiet time to say, "Talk of God is difficult for me, but I felt something else in this meeting which to me was so wonderful. I felt the closeness of all of us here to one another. I was moved to find how near and dear the rest of you seemed to me."

One may at times question the authenticity of a crowd's "love" for each other; but it would be difficult indeed to deny the deepening understanding and sense of closeness which grows so obviously as a group of people meditate together time after time.

People are meditating out of a wish to solve their problems; out of a need for healing and renewal; out of a longing to know what it is to be human; out of a need for silence and discipline, in order to maintain their own identity in a world of violent change. But we are only halfway up the ladder, for, finally, as we shall see, we meditate also for joy, for awareness of the natural world, and for spiritual growing.

CHAPTER 3

One Is All; All Is One

~~~~~~

In the depths of meditation I find out who I am; I discover the bond that ties me to my fellow men; but most of all in the peak moments of my inward journey, I catch glimpses of another and more profound unity: the unity that *binds me to the natural world*, to all created things and to the spirit of life.

One of the many such occasions in my own life stays in my mind because it helped to rid me of a long-held fear. For many years, our family has owned a summer camp in a Nova Scotia forest. It is very beautiful; but when my husband and I were there alone, I was often afraid in the silence of the night far from other people. One summer night I woke in such a silence, as usual hearing no sound at all but the tick of the old clock and the soft splash of water in the mountain brook outside the door. I lay still, as I often did when I woke in the night, staring into the dark until my eyes had grown accustomed to it, until the dark lightened and became friendlier. Outside, that night, a great full moon hung in the sky above the tall trees, and it was as though there were a playful fire in the woods.

The wind tossed the branches across the moon's path, and the world outside the window alternately brightened and darkened as the moon appeared and disappeared behind each tree and cloud. Too fascinated to be afraid, I got up, put on a robe and went out on the porch alone. The moonlight lay in the branches above the singing brook like coarse sugar piled high with a kind of pewter shimmer in the night. The wind was flowing, and the waving trees broke the light into flickering fragments.

I sat on the railing watching for a long time. There were small stirrings in the wood, but they seemed gentle and harmless. I thought with love of our kinship with all else that lives, of how profoundly we ourselves, through the chemistry and the rhythm of our bodies, are part of the natural world around us and participate in it; and at last I stepped off the porch and walked a little way under the trees.

A thin cloud passed over the moon, and one tall poplar tree turned ghostlike and then, as the moon reappeared, resumed the shape we call natural. I thought of how the forest, like all living things, was not as it appeared to be; that trees were not "solid" but full of the empty spaces between the molecules which have grouped themselves to make a tree; and that the nature of the tree was hidden from me because I see through limited eyes, and through my limited ears fail to hear the multiple sounds of its growing. I thought that in my own heart too there were hidden places because no observer had the eyes to see, the ears to hear.

I remained there in the forest a long time, and it seemed to me that I understood both the friendliness and the mystery of all living things and that I would never be afraid of the night and the silence again.

Many people experience such moments. The literature

of meditation and mysticism is full of them. Sometimes they come spontaneously, but even then it is clear that they spring from another part of ourselves, another way of consciousness. But however they come we know, for a breathless space, that there is something beyond our daily lives; for a little space of time we know how lovely is the dwelling place of God and how magically things are made, everything to its purpose.

A friend of mine acquired the habit of meditating during the long months of recovery from a serious illness; and now, when she is depressed or discouraged, she goes off by herself to renew her bond with life. "One morning last summer," she told me, "I got up at four o'clock to watch the sunrise. It was still dark and I sat alone on a log, not moving, lost in myself, trying to sense everything around me. When the sky did light up I was ready. I saw each separate leaf catch fire and I felt somehow as if I too were lighting up, as if we all came out of the dark together, as if we all moved in the same rhythm."

What we remember with joy from such experiences is the sense of *unity*, the feeling that we are a part of all that lives. The very stones and hills seem vividly alive; we find a meaning in everything—the seed in the ground, the bark on the tree, the sound of the cricket. We feel that there is something out there which is identical with something in ourselves. "Here all blades of grass, wood and stone, all things are one," exulted the great fourteenth-century German mystic Johannes Eckhart.

It is a unity not unlike that which people feel for each other at the peak of love, a sense that that which is in me is in you too; a pattern running through life, through the little and the big—the acorn and the stars, the piping of the sparrow and the majesty of the carillon in the great cathedral, the bee laboring in the flower and the genius at his desk—a continuity from the lowly amoeba to the great orchestra of the human brain. Truth is "flowing like an eternal spring," cried a Japanese meditator; and in his book *On the Psychology of Meditation* Brazilian psychologist Claudio Naranjo declares: "To the extent that we are 'ourselves,' we are also a part of the cosmos, a tide in the ocean of life, a chain in the network of processes that do not either begin or end within the enclosure of our skins."

Of such a moment John Cowper Powys wrote eloquently that "nothing grows upon the earth; nothing flies through the air or swims in the sea but is linked by some subtle magnetic link to the lonely life of our own soul." There is a feeling that life is whole; I and my world are part of each other; I and all life are united in the bond of love and understanding.

Such knowledge often comes spontaneously—as suddenly as lightning comes in the heat of a summer day. The late Abraham Maslow—the Brandeis University psychologist whose long research into what he called "peak experiences" gave a great deal of the impetus to the inward revolution—reported hundreds of such spontaneous experiences among the people he studied, and he came to the conclusion that such experiences happened to all of us at one time or another. Describing them as they were reported to him, he wrote: "All separateness and distance from the world disappeared as they felt one with the world, fused with it, really belonging in it and to it, instead of being outside looking in. . . . There was a *oneness* where there was a twoness, an integration of some sort of the self with the non-self."

We are startled in the peak experience by this "at-oneness"; but we are also startled by the sudden beauty and marvel of what we are seeing. For a single instant we know the loveliness, the intricacy, the importance of all living things; a flower petal, a bird's wing, the root of a tree—everything we see is suddenly beautiful beyond measure, soaked and drenched with radiant life.

Such experience can indeed be as seemingly spontaneous as a rainbow; but it can also be the fruition of disciplined meditation. Meditation often brings an increase in the quality and depth of our awareness, and, in fact, experienced meditators believe that the end product of meditation for most people is increased awareness—awareness not only of ourselves but of the world around us.

Certainly it is one of the major goals of people who practice that summit of meditation called *contemplation.* Contemplation, its practitioners tell us, is seeing things as they really are, as they appear to poets and children—brimming with light and color, growing and changing.

The Buddhists call it "recollection—or constant awareness of the immediate present." And in Zen one speaks of seeing something the five-hundredth time in the same way one saw it the first time. Scott Crom, a distinguished Quaker and professor of philosophy at Beloit College, puts it this way: "Meditation is not an intellectual activity but an increase in the over-all quality and depth of our total awareness." And a Catholic contemplative, Father William McNamara, defines contemplation as "the highest possible focus of human attention on the present moment or the present being."

How rarely it happens to us! The peak experiences, whether they come spontaneously or are sought through the discipline of meditation, are the special moments of life. For the most part we pass unseeing through the magic and mystery of living, blind to reality, walking through miracles every day without even noticing. It is as though we moved through the world in a palanquin, curtains drawn, being carried through the forests, under the stars, beside the sea, while inside, unseeing, we scribbled advertising copy, totaled up accounts, planned investments or polished the furniture.

To know how far one has fallen from the profound awareness of contemplation one has only to remember the way a bonfire of autumn leaves smelled when we were children; or how it felt to crunch through snow or fly a kite, or dive into cool water on a hot summer day. As we grow older we let go of the eternal moment, the "now," and with that loss we let reality itself slip through our fingers. For outside the prison we make for ourselves there is another kind of a world, different in its wholeness, different in its significance, different in the particularity of leaf, and cloud, and the intricate branches of bare November trees.

In that world there is a meaning in everything—the seed in the ground, the bark on the tree, the small evening sound of the cricket. Every cloud and shadow, even the very stones and hills, are vividly alive. There is sometimes a sense that everything is flowing—the wind in the leaves, the water on the shore, the clouds in the sky—and that nothing is unimportant. One is reminded of the famous line from the poet William Blake, "If the doors of perception were cleansed, everything would appear to man as it is, infinite."

People long for such awareness. We often try risk and danger to return us to the sharpened sense of the now. We ski from great heights, pilot small planes, sail a boat through storm and wind, or live alone pitting our skills against the wilderness, all for the sake of feeling alive and aware. Writing in *Ascent*, the journal of the Sierra Club, Doug Robinson quotes a visionary mountain climber, Alan Steck of the Hummingbird Ridge Club. Steck said that as he was ascending Mount Logan he turned for a moment and was "completely lost in a silent appraisal of the beautifully sensuous simplicity of windblown snow . . ., the form and motion of the blowing snow . . . Only a moment," he said, "and yet by virtue of total absorption [the climber] is lost in it and the winds of eternity blow through it."*

The longing has always been there. It is enhanced now by our long urban separation from the natural world and because for so long we have been seeing nature as ours to manipulate and even destroy. This is part of the reason for the sudden rise of interest in ecology. Ecologists and meditators have much in common. Pragmatically, empirically, the ecologist knows what the meditator long ago discovered in the depth of his own heart—that there *is* a unity in all things. "As human beings we have our roots in nature," wrote Rollo May,

> not simply because of the fact that the chemistry of our bodies is of essentially the same elements as the air or dirt or grass. In a multitude of other ways we participate in nature—the rhythm of the change of seasons or of night and day, for example, is reflected in the rhythm of our bodies, of hunger and fulfillment, of sleep and wakefulness, of sexual desire and gratification, and in countless other ways.

* Doug Robinson, "The Climber as Visionary," *Ascent,* The Sierra Club Mountaineering Journal, Vol. 64, No. 3, May 1969.

Meditation by itself cannot compel the moment of awareness; but it teaches openness, waiting, stillness; it peels off the layers of unbelief and helps exorcise the spirit of rationalism, of scientism, and in its place teaches an embracing tenderness for the world of other living things.

Perhaps this feeling of oneness comes because when we meditate we go down into the collective unconscious, the stream we share with all men. Or perhaps the kingdom of heaven *is* within us; perhaps there is a linkage between our minds and whatever governs the world. At any rate, in our inward-conscious world we have given our feelings about it a contemporary name. The sense that we are at one with a never-ceasing flow of life is one of the many experiences which scientists call "altered states of consciousness."

But beautiful as such awareness is, it is not yet the mountaintop. The ultimate goal of meditation—said by those who reach it to be the utmost level of human existence—is *enlightenment*. Buddhists call it "satori"; Christians call it "the practice of the presence of God"; and in our day Carlos Castaneda picturesquely defined it as "passing through the crack that leads to the other world."

It is a state of conscious unity with ultimate reality, a reality in and beyond both nature and our reaching, longing selves; and it is called "enlightenment" because in that unity the experiencing individual feels he has encountered truth—truth clear and indisputable—about the nature of the universe, God and the human soul. Here, says Al-Ghazali, most famous of the Sufis of Islam, "mortals reach the end of their ascent."

It has been described in many ways by people who have emerged from it awestruck and changed. It is, they have said, that point in the mind where "the timeless intersects with time." It is "the suprasensory, suprarational level of mental activity that transcends all other human experiences." It is "the still point of the turning world."

Maslow too reported on it. He said, "There is universally reported a seeing of formerly hidden truth, a revelation in the strict sense, a stripping away of veils, and finally, almost always, the whole experience is experienced as bliss, ecstasy, rapture, exaltation."

It is also, of course, what the mystics call "the encounter with God"—the Biblical "Be still and know that I am God." After long study of the literature of such experience, Dr. Dean—who says he has never himself had such experience but describes it nonetheless with great accuracy —writes: "A noetic illumination that is quite impossible to describe occurs. In an intuitive flash one has an awareness of the meaning and drift of the universe, an identification and merging with creation, infinity and immortality, a depth beyond revealed meaning—in short, a conception of an 'Over-Self' so omnipotent that religion has interpreted it as God."

Not only the Scriptures but the literature of the ages is full of the story of such experiences. One picks and chooses among thousands, all different yet all startlingly similar. The year after he graduated from college, wrote the Quaker mystic Rufus Jones, he was in France near the foothills of the Alps.

I was walking alone in a forest, trying to map out my plan of life and confronted with issues which seemed too complex and difficult for my mind to solve. Suddenly I felt the walls between the visible and the invisible grow thin and the Eternal seemed to break through into the world where I was. I saw no flood of light, I heard no voice, but I felt as though I were face to face with a higher order of reality than that of the trees or mountains. I went down on my knees there in the woods with the same feeling of awe which compelled men in earlier times to take off their shoes from their feet. A sense of mission broke in on me and I felt that I was being called to a well-defined task of life to which I then and there dedicated myself.

Thomas Merton, the Trappist monk who was perhaps the most renowned solitary of our time, wrote eloquently of a similar experience:

Our souls rise up from our earth like Jacob waking from his dream and exclaiming: "Truly God is in this place and I knew it not!" God himself becomes the only reality in Whom all other reality takes its proper place—and falls into insignificance. . . . A door opens in the center of our being and we seem to fall through it into immense depths which, although they are infinite, are all accessible to us; all eternity seems to have become ours in this one placid and breathless contact."

The late Rabbi Abraham Heschel, whose life of compassionate service was balanced by deep spiritual experience, wrote:

A moment comes like a thunderbolt, in which a flash of the undisclosed rends our dark apathy asunder. It is full of overpowering brilliance, like a point in which all moments of life are focused or a thought which outweighs all thoughts ever conceived of. There is so much light in our cage, in our world, it is as if it were suspended amidst the stars. Apathy turns to splendor unawares. The ineffable has shuddered itself into the soul. . . . We are penetrated by His insight. We cannot think any more as if He were there and we here. He is both there and here. He is not a *being,* but *being in and beyond all beings.*

These are the experiences of Christians and Jews. The Eastern religions, of course, can add enough to fill a mammoth library. Philip Kapleau, a former American businessman who gave up his business to study Zen Buddhism and after twelve years of study and practice was ordained a Zen priest, describes satori—which Zen teachers often refer to as self-realization. It is afternoon and he has come for a formal interview with the roshi—a title which means "venerable teacher"—his Zen master. Having been warned by his teacher that he is close to his goal, he has devoted the previous twenty-four hours to a meditation so absorbed that it went on even as he ate and swept floors. Now the master begins his instruction. But he has said only a few words, says Kapleau, when

> all at once the roshi, the room, every single thing disappeared in a dazzling stream of illumination and I felt myself bathed in a delicious, unspeakable delight. . . . For a fleeting eternity I was alone—I was alone . . . Then the roshi swam into view. Our eyes met and flowed into each other, and we burst out laughing . . . "I have it! [cried Kapleau]! I know. . . . There is nothing, absolutely nothing. I am everything and everything is nothing."

So numerous are these occasions and so frequently do they happen to people of wisdom and nobility that it would be the height of arrogance to disbelieve their existence. But how does one come to this pure and absolute height?

Sometimes swiftly and spontaneously. I remember an experience of my own years ago. I was flying over the Midwest on a spring day. Below the plane an unbroken floor of shining clouds stretched from horizon to horizon. So clearly were the cloud formations delineated that it was as though one looked out on a landscape complete with bays and rivers, hills and valleys, jutting cliffs and quiet meadows. Suddenly, with that falling away of material surroundings so characteristic of the mystic experience, I found myself, as it were, released from the plane and its occupants, moving with confidence on the floor of clouds. The emotional texture of the experience was one of the greatest contentment and radiance, and with it came in staggering certainty that knowledge of the nature of the light which made the English poet Rupert Brooke describe it as "light more alive than you."

Here in the presence of this light it seemed to me that there could never be loneliness, nor would human beings as such ever be needed again. The thing we call human was in the light itself, and the warmth of human tenderness—I suddenly knew—was not focused alone in the corporeal creature we call man but was part of the very fabric, the very life of the universe.

The experience was unforgettable, and it left behind the compelling certainty that the *form* in which we dwell in this life or another is unimportant, for we dwell safely in a universe far more personal, far more human, far more tender than we are.

But though it may come spontaneously, meditation has long been a charted road to the top of the mountain. "Spiritual teachers of all ages have been unanimous in de-

claring that we can come to know God through meditation," writes John White. Meditation can bring us to an
awareness of the living world; and with one more step, it
can take us to the borders of that invisible world which
haunts us all our lives like the perfume of unseen roses.

Certainly mystic symbols frequently appear in the
course of meditation, even for people without training. I
think of another experience of my own. For several years
a group of employees of the United Nations has been
meeting for meditation once a week, and on one such occasion I joined them. The group of about thirty or forty
people was led by Sri Chinmoy, who is described as a
spiritual master and yogi. For an hour, we sat in silence—
a silence punctuated only by a deep-throated *"Om"* from
the "pulpit" and by the almost soundless movements of
the monk pacing among us. The time seemed short and
the surroundings unimportant. In fact, I found myself
part of a scene alien to daily experience. I seemed to be
sitting on a narrow shoreline. Behind me an unscalable
cliff rose sharp and straight. Between me and the sea, an
ethereal child ran lightly as thistledown, barely touching
the ground, and then vanished, still dancing, on the crest
of a wave. I burrowed into the warm sand, and from the
cliff yellow roses fell in showers. The air seemed full of
what I can only call Presence. Under me I felt the pulse
of the earth as a slow, regular, reassuring lullaby.

Organized religion is greatly indebted to its mystics,
whose relationship to the church is like that of the theoretical scientist to applied science. Appropriately, it was
Einstein, the greatest scientific theorist, who said of religion: "To know that what is impenetrable to us really
exists, manifesting itself as the highest wisdom and the
most radiant beauty which our dull faculties can compre-

hend only in their primitive forms—this knowledge, this feeling is at the center of true religiousness."

Such overwhelming experience is the gift of the great mystics. But we should not forget that though most of us will never endure the long and disciplined years that lead to satori, or bring the monk in his cell an ineffable moment, the sudden sense of a Presence of "holiness that hovers over all things" is an experience that happens to vast numbers of people. "I strongly suspect that there is something close to an instinct for transcendence in human beings," writes sociologist Peter Berger. And Dr. Jean Houston, who with her husband Robert Masters heads the Foundation for Mind Research, has concluded on the basis of the hundreds of experiments she and her husband have conducted that the brain-mind system has "a congenital point of contact with something that is experienced as God, as a fundamental reality or as the most Holy."

Mystic enlightenment and meditation are not the same thing. But experts who study both phenomena believe that meditation paves the way for such experience because it helps open and stretch our minds to new dimensions, and because it distracts us from the endless data which floods in on us from outside. Here is the stairway, the journey to the mountaintop, the utmost reward of meditation —what Dr. Dean calls "the ultraconscious summit." "Miraculous powers have been attributed to the ultraconscious," writes Dr. Dean, "and from it have sprung the highest creativity and loftiest ideals known to man." From it also have come our most unforgettable *chronicles of joy*.

It is a surprise to find that our "real" selves, when they appear, seem to be naturally joyous. After satori, Philip Kapleau wrote, "I feel free as a fish swimming in an ocean

of cool, clear water, after being stuck in a tank of glue
. . . and so grateful for everything. . . . But mostly I am
grateful for my human body, for the privilege as a human
being to know this Joy, like no other."

Joy indeed saturates the descriptions of this summit experience. From the daily practitioners of the rather simple
ritual of Transcendental Meditation to the monk who has
plunged into satori, the theme song is consistently Joy.
"What is this joy I feel? Who shall measure it? I know
nothing but joy, limitless, unbounded," cried the Eastern
mystic Shankara. And Saint Augustine asked himself a
question, "What do I love when I love Thee?," and gave
what one commentator called a "mind-blowing answer":
"A kind of light and melody and fragrance and food and
embracement—of my inner man. Where there shines into
my soul what space cannot contain, and there sounds
what time snatches not away, and where there is fragrance which no breeze disperses."

It happened so to me one morning recently. I had been
in deep depression the night before, feeling agnostic,
weary, full of failure, and lay awake trying to dispel the
miasma of gloom with deep meditation. I still was depressed when I went down to my desk, but was suddenly
visited by a profound, wildly exciting experience—not the
mysticism in which time, space and world vanish, but the
kind which has to be called the experience of God. Joy
and glory seemed to pour with the sun through the windows on my face so that I threw my head back, longing to
be a vessel into which it could flow forever.

In my journal for that day I struggled to describe what
had happened to me. "Through the Dead Sea," I wrote,
"through the salty, gray, arid desert, I go into the high-
lands and the sun—oh, the glory of the light! Is it outside

or inside? A darkness is lifted; the light has broken through; a dam has broken and the sweet waters are pouring in."

This enormous joy has happened to many other people. Some time ago I shared the platform at a book-author luncheon with Peter Putnam, a young man who, in despair, had attempted suicide with sleeping pills and was blinded as a result. Nevertheless, he had written what was apparently a joyous book, called *Cast Off the Darkness*. Moved by his comments on it, I went home to read it and found this description of his convalescent days:

Life was utterly simple, having no aim but its own self-renewal. I left the world and its business to others. My business was to get well. At many moments I was as spiritually alone, as oblivious of time, as devoid of conscious thought, as during that unremembered ten-day sleep. I felt a mystic intuition of resurgent life, glowing and tangible within me, the most perfect peace and joy that I had ever known.

. . . Each transition from desolation to exaltation was simply the triumphant affirmation of resurgent life, a rebirth, and a new beginning. Each was a repetition on a smaller scale of the underlying conflict between my will for death by suicide and the overwhelming joy of life that all those years had dwelt within me unsuspected. I do not know and shall never know at what exact hour and minute within my ten-day sleep I stumbled upon this priceless treasure, but I do know that in that instant my life launched on its true beginning.

Such joy may surprise some people, since meditation is thought of as an exercise in quietness. But inner space is also wild, diverse, beautiful, eventful, and it is really true that the further we go into ourselves, the closer we come to joy. Long ago the philosopher Plotinus wrote: "There is always a radiance in the soul of man, untroubled, like the light in a lantern in a wild turmoil of rain and tempest."

Where does it come from? Why does it come? Who knows? The kingdom of heaven within? The freedom to be yourself, the shedding of the chains of hectic daily life, the marshaling of the resources of mind and body, the coming to the true self, the experience of God? Someone once said, "Joy is the echo of God's life in you."

Who knows? At any rate the joy is real. In fact simply because it is a greater joy—a better high—than drugs, meditation has been used very effectively against drug addiction. After long experience with drug addicts and drug usage, psychologist Andrew Weil now says, "The highs of meditation are universally perceived as better than drug highs."

In the end the most important happenings of our lives are the ones that occur in what Jacques Maritain called "the invisible universe which is the mind of man." Meditation is a powerful means of transformation from the turbulent, distracted self to the whole and healthy one. And it turns out also that the human beings most likely to grow are those who are in conscious contact with the inner world as well as with the world without.

"I'm not healing sickness or experiencing satori or anything like that," one young meditator told me. "I'm just learning to be a better, happier, more useful person." That is good; but there is more than that. The inner self is, after all, the arena where the great moral battles are fought, where conscience is illuminated, where clues are floated about the purpose and meaning of life; and it is clearly a source of energy and power.

Speaking from a psychoanalyst's standpoint, Dr. James Hillman says that "through living in rather than only acting out, immense instinctual energy is given to inner life." I remember Dr. Maslow telling me that peak experience in some cases removes neurotic symptoms forever. In one of his articles he has written: "To know the universe is all of a piece and that one has his place in it—one is part of it, belongs in it—can be so profound and uprooting an experience that it can change them forever." And he added that one of his subjects had had "strong, obsessional thoughts of suicide" and had been cured, "totally, immediately and permanently cured," through the transformation of a peak experience.

Meditation bridges the span between what we are and what we'd like to be, induces the miracle of rebirth—the endless process of creating the Self which is the demand that life makes on every man. It is in truth a journey to ourselves, for the Self is not what we think it is, but instead a continuation of the flower, the substance, the grief, and the growing of the universe.

Meditation is also a discoverer of the ideals by which we live and the ethical concepts which give our lives significance. And it goes on for a lifetime, for the inner self grows neither old nor tired nor jaded. When life approaches its close, we will have learned to find wisdom and strength within ourselves, in the austere and noble loneliness of a mature mind, or we will have not found it at all.

CHAPTER 4

The Quiet Revolution

~~~~~~

Meditation's credentials are as ancient and authentic as time itself, and its sudden reappearance in the twentieth century is profoundly interesting. The forms that reappearance takes are even more so. Were they only repetitions of the past they would be important enough, coming as they do after the long and sterile years. But in fact they are often salty, unique, contemporary, full of the inventiveness of a technological age. So let us take a look now in detail at the panorama of a novel revolution which, for good or for bad, is shaping our lives, overthrowing old beliefs, changing our ways of thinking and doing, loving and being.

It is morning—midmorning—in the high desert of Arizona, and the sun is bright and hot. It shines on the great red conical mountains standing, separate and mysterious as pyramids, as startling as Stonehenge, amongst the sagebrush and the century trees and the tall dried stalks of yucca. There is silence everywhere—total silence except for a single bird which incessantly repeats one note. Not a leaf stirs. Even the dry, yellowish grasses are still.

I am not entirely alone. There is a swing near me, a rope swing like a child's, and a young man sits on it reading. He looks up and we smile at each other, but we do not speak. Morning here is not the time for speaking. A girl in shorts and bare feet goes by playing a guitar very softly and singing. She passes in front of me, not seeing me. She is going down to the gate, and I follow. A sign glitters in the sun on the wooden bars of the gate. It reads: "Nada Contemplative Center—All Who Enter Here, No Fuss."

In fact there is no fuss—only silence and peace. I am not surprised, because I knew before I arrived at this Catholic but ecumenical center, also called the Spiritual Life Institute, that it existed for a single purpose, "to call contemporary Americans of all faiths to share the contemplative experience."

It is three days now since I arrived on a night of impenetrable starless darkness, after a long journey over precipitous mountains in a bus whose driver was, of all things, a moonlighting monk. A blue-jeaned girl met me and guided me across the shadowed, sleeping ranch to my "house." Almost by touch we found a door and then a light switch. Inside there were small high windows—out of which nothing could be seen in the dark—a chair or two, some cluttered shelves, a bed, a cupboard with crackers, peanut butter, an orange, instant coffee, cups, plate and knife; a bathroom of sorts, which could be reached only by going out on a kind of patio. There was also no discoverable way to lock the door, and I lay in the silence for some time full of urban fancies, waiting for the handle to turn, for the footsteps of danger in the night.

I am in a less austere cottage now, but the silence is here still, profound and somehow joyful. I have been here three days. This morning I did not go to six-o'clock chapel. Instead, with the ringing of the bell still in my ears, I went into the desert to see the sun rise. The bird—the solitary bird—was singing then too, over and over the same note. Then silence fell—silence, silence, silence. I broke it at last saying aloud, because I could not help it, "The Lord is in His holy temple. Let all the earth keep silent before Him."

I don't yet know what is happening to me here, but I know that time seems to vanish, to have no existence. One discovers with surprise that hot and cold matter little; that peanut butter and crackers are a fine substitute for orange juice and coffee at breakfast time; that it is good to rise at five and, best of all, good to be silent amongst other silent people; good to spend an hour studying a lizard on the rocks or a red mountain changing lights in the hot sun.

Let us go back now across the country. It's a bitterly cold winter night and I am shivering. I am standing in a queue of people outside a not yet opened door on New York's East Side. A modest plaque on the door says this is the Zen Studies Society, Inc. A young man next to me in the line says he's been coming to meetings here for a long time. He has read many of the writings of Suzuki, the great Japanese Zen master who taught at Columbia University in the early years of the century. He has been looking for a place to experience the teachings of this cele-brated philosopher and has found it here in a dignified place of study, which was, in fact, founded to provide a working center for Dr. Suzuki.

He asks why I am there, and I tell him I am writing a book about meditation. He says he knows three people who are also writing books about it. He says everyone he knows is into it.

The door must be opening, because the line is surging ahead. It is precisely six-thirty, the appointed hour. We go into a small anteroom, where we surrender our shoes and other belongings. Even purses, to my alarm, are taken away.

Beginners like me are led upstairs to our own special room. It is a long, narrow, beige-walled bare room, with a great row of black cushions running down each side. We are directed, without speech, to sit cross-legged on the cushions, facing the wall, and are also somehow made aware that we sit in meditation. After a while a gentle-voiced Western woman in Buddhist robes takes her place on a cushion at the end of the room and tells us how to sit in lotus position; how to clasp our hands together; how to breathe, counting one on the inhale, two on the exhale and so forth; how to clasp our hands under the abdomen and feel the breath there, feel also a "mind" there.

We sit in total silence a long time; the street sounds outside seem no more intrusive than the rustling of trees on a summer day while one is dozing or reading.

But at last there is a break in our "Zen-sitting," and we start "Zen-walking," forming lines, eyes straight ahead, feet rising and falling. We march downstairs through the much more prestigious classroom of the established students, where the Buddha sits, shadowed against the wall, out into a cold, dark, empty room, through the open doorway of which one can see a patch of white-stone "garden," and then through a narrow, dark, tunnellike hallway with brick walls.

Back in the room with the higher-grade students, we listen to a robed monk, gentle and witty, who tells us what we have been doing and why. We chant briefly. From time to time there is the sharp sound of a gong.

Then the evening is over and I realize incredulously that I have been sitting, if not in full lotus, then at least cross-legged on the floor for the best part of three hours. I have been too conscious of the pain of this unfamiliar posture to feel really lost in meditation. But I have forgotten, totally forgotten, my fear when my belongings were taken from me. I have also forgotten the problems I brought in with me; and I have spent these three hours in a world of great gentleness, compassion and dignity.

There were many older people like myself in this reverent, quiet group; but the gathering was predominantly young. There are, in fact, many young people in all these movements of discovery. Sometimes they *are* the movement.

I am thinking, for example, of an early spring evening in Denver, Colorado. The lobby of the Sheraton-Cadillac is full of the usual evening people checking in at theater counters, trailing down the stairs in tuxedos and evening gowns, gathering in the bars.

But at the entrance of the ballroom a different crowd is gathering, a huge crowd of young people: girls in long Mother Hubbards, blue jeans, ponchos; long-haired boys with smiling faces. It is an hour yet before the doors will open, but they are there anyhow, trying to get a seat up front where they can see at close hand the young Maharaj Ji, who is, for them, the emissary of God.

Some have come a long way. It is rumored that there are busloads from Arizona and even farther away. While they wait they are silent for the most part, eyes closed, apparently obeying their leader's injunction to "meditate, meditate."

Finally they are allowed inside, and in moments the

great auditorium is packed with hundreds of young people. There will be a long wait still, for the young Maharaj is almost never on time. A rock band plays; small children wander on and off the platform. The musicians depart, and a curly-haired young man gets up and announces that when the candles are lit it means that the Maharaj has left his residence and is on his way.

At last more young men enter, and the candelabrum glows with light. People shout and clap their hands in rhythm. They sing,

> The Lord of the universe
> Has come to us this day;
> And he's bound to show us the way.

They rise, and some put their arms around each other; some join hands instead and raise their joined hands; some stand on chairs. They are enraptured and grow steadily more so. A young mother joyously tosses a beaming baby. Now, surprisingly, they sing the Christian hymn "And they'll know us by our love." As it finishes, a dark plump young man comes in, smiling a little as he faces the crowd. He is wearing a dark suit, and he looks much older than his age. He speaks, not particularly well. His voice rises and falls like an old-time minister's; but it is expressive, as are his gestures.

What he is saying is apparently what he says in one form or another every time. Everything in life is worth giving up for the Knowledge, the Knowledge of God, which he is ready to give to whoever asks for it with a guileless heart. If they will but come to him, the Knowledge is theirs for the asking. For the rest: meditate, meditate. I feel little empathy; but the young people—an astonishing number of them are college graduates—gaze at him with longing, love and reverence and, when he has left the platform, pour out shining-eyed into a lobby which is still full of curious and apparently skeptical people.

On an impulse, I speak to one of the latter—a fortyish business-type man picking up his *New York Times* at the newsstand. He is glad to talk, and full of curiosity.

"What are they doing?" he asks.

"They say," I tell him, "that they are looking for the Knowledge of God; they are being 'blissed out'; they are learning to meditate."

"Well, I can identify with that," he says. "My wife and I spent our vacation at a mountain commune with some old friends who have gone there to live. We spent a lot of time meditating. It's a good thing. I found out a great deal about myself and a great deal about my friends too."

In fact, though the turn to inwardness began with millions of searching, seeking young people, adult meditators now seem almost as sold on the benefits of silence and inwardness as the young. For example, they comprised almost all of the people who gathered on a windy March day in a modernistic Unitarian church in Hartford, Connecticut. They had come for a whole-day session of meditation and healing, a session sponsored by the Spiritual Frontiers Fellowship.

The Fellowship was established by clergy and laymen within the conventional church's membership. It is one of several groups which have sprung up within the churches in an attempt, as SFF puts it, "to open the eyes of a materialistic and skeptical generation to man's intrinsic spiritual nature." An organization on their own, they nevertheless hold their meetings in churches whenever possible; indeed, the group is made up almost entirely of church members and clergymen.

Each local group decides on its own format, and today the Central Connecticut group is holding a day-long seminar of healing and meditation, led by the Reverend John Scudder, a somewhat controversial and certainly interesting figure. Formerly an engineer, Scudder, who believes he cured himself of cancer, is now a minister, pastor of the esoteric Pyramid of Light Church in Richton Park, Illinois, and he is supposed to have cured many people with meditation, prayer and the laying on of hands.

The basement room where the meeting is held today is octagonal and bare and contains no symbols of a church. There are probably a hundred people here, and they are talking informally in small groups. I join one of these and ask people who have been with Scudder before whether he has cured anyone. "Oh, yes," they tell me; and one woman says, "A young girl was cured of cancer last time." Others report that they "felt so much better" after the meeting.

Except that they *believe*, there is nothing to distinguish these people from any other group in the church or out of it. Talking with them at intermission, I encountered a couple of artists, a school social worker, a sculptor, an insurance executive, a YMCA director, a singer, a doctor, an engineer, a dental hygienist.

Scudder has come in now. He is a very thin man with the sunken eyes, at once brilliant and dreamlike, which I am discovering often among saints and seers. He is making a speech, and the people listen absorbedly. He speaks most of the day, off and on, and the promised small groups do not materialize; but he shows us how to meditate—for faith healing or for any other purpose. Under his instructions we exhale, inhale, counting as we do, and try many other exercises, including sending energy to the heart while, with hand on pulse, we feel "the rising of the energy." Spiritual development first, he says, and then psychic development. He quotes Jesus' "Seek ye first the kingdom of heaven and its righteousness and all these things shall be added unto you"; and he reminds us that one of the gifts recorded in the New Testament is the miracle of healing.

He says that sometimes he meditates for ten or twenty hours while seeking healing for someone. The point is to break through no matter how long it takes, and he promises, "You will know it when it happens."

There are no visible cures today, though we pray for them. In the end, we form a "healing circle," a huge circle in which we stand holding one another's hands. Mr. Scudder prays and we sing, "God be with you till we meet again," and then stand in silence waiting for a blessing; and there *is* a kind of electricity. Perhaps it comes from each one to another. Perhaps it emanates from the gaunt man facing us. Certainly he is an impressive figure, ascetic in appearance and seemingly devout, and, like the many other spiritual healers of this remarkable century, he raises questions which, I suspect, we will all be trying to answer in the decades to come.

But the most adventurous journey is still ahead of us. Come with me to a small town up the Hudson River not far from New York. Here on a hilltop is a huge rambling house, painted blue, surrounded by a shaggy yard full of dogs and cats. Inside you wander about like Alice in Wonderland, from one strange beguiling room to the next, seventeen in all. You can lose your way without trouble; but you won't mind, because there is so much to see. There are thousands of books, including the contents of a huge bookcase in the bathroom. There are many kinds of ancient artifacts. A huge, circular, feathered mandala hangs on one wall; there is a mummy case in the living room; small statues of gods abound, including one of the potent Egyptian goddess Sekhmet.

Among these ancient racial memories, there are some very contemporary objects indeed. There are "enabling" devices for enlarging and releasing the mind's capacities; biofeedback machines; a device with a keyboard on which you can produce scores of different kinds of sounds and blends of sounds; colored slides designed to help produce altered states of consciousness; a modern version of the ancient witch's cradle in which an experimenter can swing and spin; paintings of microscopic objects, cunningly contrived and enlarged to remind one of, or even to induce, altered states of consciousness.

There are also stroboscopic lights, video equipment, visual environments of all kinds. There are rooms where a would-be meditator can be locked in darkness and silence, and other rooms where groups of meditators meet for "mind games"—guided meditations which take one even deeper and deeper into the inner Self.

A witch's cave? A spiritualist's haven? No; the Foundation for Mind Research, the center run by Robert Masters and Jean Houston. Both are Ph.D.s and both are supported in part by grants from a variety of foundations. What they are trying to do is so important that we will hear more about it as the book goes on; briefly, they are seeking to find nondrug ways of inducing altered states of consciousness, ways which may range from sensory deprivation to induced trance.

These stories are taken from legions of possible ones. So vast, in fact, is the movement that it would take a lifetime to read the contemporary literature and to visit all the hundreds of centers of meditation. They range all the way from the Nyingma Institute in California, where a Tibetan monk in exile, a scholar of distinction, leads a dual program of meditation and of scholarly instruction in history and philosophy, to living-room gatherings, meeting with self-taught gurus. Some offer little more than outlandish novelty and vanish as fast as they come; some seem more interested in money than in wisdom; some appear to be made up largely of naïve followers, people who are ready to snatch at any fashionable fad.

But no one can travel among them without being aware also of a great congeries of brilliant, searching minds, seeking the unifying thread of life, the meaning and context of human existence. One thinks of the new Quaker communes where young people of that sapient faith seek ways of combining spiritual growth and action; of Dialogue House in New York, where, under the direction of psychotherapist Ira Progoff, director of the Institute for Research in Depth Psychology at the Graduate School of Drew University and founder-director of Dialogue House, people spend seminar weekends in a process of steadily growing self-knowledge through an interior dialogue with themselves, with other people, with God, and through the keeping of a journal, a log of spiritual change.

One thinks of Kirkridge, a retreat led by John Oliver Nelson—for years a professor at Yale Divinity School—and his wife, Jane, both ministers. In a rambling homey group of buildings high up in the top of the Pocono Mountains in Pennsylvania, they welcome annually doctors and lawyers, housewives and teachers, writers and monks, mediums and teen-agers, scientists and ministers.

Some of these people come for the numerous seminars

on marriage and on problems of the contemporary world. But great numbers come also for the Deepening Retreats, which are of all sorts: an experiential session on "withdrawal in depth" led by the distinguished Quaker Douglas Steere; a seminar which explores the concepts of biofeedback, dream interpretation, psychic phenomena; a retreat conducted by Dr. Nelson himself centering on Celtic mysticism, worship, sainthood and "the joyous art forms of Lindisfarne and Iona"; a discussion led by a young man just back from India, where he was researching a Ph.D. in anthropology, centering his research on Asian and Western spiritual heritages—on Hindu, Tibetan, Buddhist and Hebrew paths to the one God.

Like a great wind, the longing for inwardness blows across the country, overthrowing old values, creating new understandings, changing our previously formed images of reality, running the gamut of human creativity. Growing swiftly, it takes in people of every age and walk of life. Businessmen and housewives, teen-agers, mystics, reformed drug addicts, scholars, psychologists and clergymen become unlikely allies, joined to one another by an urge to turn inward in search of a sense of life they have not yet found in the world around them.

Often it is religiously oriented. People involved in Eastern faiths now total in the millions, plus innumerable fellow travelers. Just about all of these groups employ meditative techniques—notably Zen Buddhism, the best-known import and one of the oldest.

Western faiths too have reasserted ancient claims. One hears of Christian communes using meditation as the core of their life together; of Hasidic communities formed by young Jews in San Francisco and Boston with spiritual renewal as their base.

Many church groups are adopting the traditional waiting silence of the Quakers. Some churches actually follow Quaker patterns. In many others, services begin and end with meditation. Some simply invite their congregations to remain silent after a service, searching their hearts for what it has meant to them. The Charismatic Renewal movement, grown from ninety people in 1967 to hundreds of thousands, now often features healing and, like the Quakers, a waiting for the spirit of God. Small groups of church members often meet in the coffeehouses of churches or in the living rooms of members in a quest for immediate religious experience through silence and meditation. In California, Episcopal Bishop C. Kilmer Myers, successor to Bishop James A. Pike, was quoted as saying that if he had his way he would remove all the chairs from San Francisco's Grace Cathedral, turn it into a meditation center and leave it open day and night. Catholic retreat houses welcome an ever-increasing number of Protestant clergymen and laity, and Protestant retreat centers are increasingly common.

Eastern and Christian faiths now often cross lines in America, searching in each other's rituals for both techniques and vision. Quakers learn Buddhist ways of worship, and in a Catholic college, Bellarmine School of Theology in Chicago, Jesuit Robert Oakes demands an hour of meditation, part of it Zen, from his students before he begins his class in spiritual awareness. Another American priest, the Reverend William Johnston, who lives and works in Japan, lectures on the mysticism of Zen to Japanese Christian converts and, back in this country, leads seminary students in the same techniques. In northern New York State, a Catholic priest operates a Center for Spiritual Studies where Buddhists, Hindus, Jews and

Christians, participating, learn meditation from each other. And at the United Nations meditation meeting I saw the leader lay loving hands on the head of a young American wearing a shirt with the face of Jesus stamped on it. Worship in communes is frequently a blend of Eastern and Christian faiths, and I was not surprised to meet one of the Maharaj Ji's staff at a Quaker meeting in the Midwest.

But people who are not religiously oriented at all are also deep in meditation. The new ways of thinking leap across the nation, appearing in very unlikely places, joining in surprising alliances. Business concerns sponsor contemplative retreats. Large corporations conduct sensitivity classes and try to induce an inward search among their employees. Public buildings set aside areas for meditation. Artists too, and musicians, are caught up in the movement, and sculptors design places for meditation. In fact, I encountered one who had constructed sixteen "contemplative environments," hideaways just big enough to enter.

An institution intended for the study of meditation, and called the University of the Trees, offers a three-year course of studies in Boulder Creek, California. In Guilford, Connecticut, an organization named the Phenix Club springs up under the direction of celebrated author Jerome Ellison. Its intent: to seek to improve the quality of the life of people, middle-aged and older, by reading, discussion, contemplation, and to emphasize the philosophical and spiritual requirements of the second half of life.

Organizations more loosely connected to the new movement abound. There is a Society for Art, Religion and Culture; an American Teilhard de Chardin Association;

an International Herman Hesse Society; a Sekhmet Institute for the Study of Images and Symbols; a Society for the Scientific Study of Religion; and many others.

The movement forms the core around which many communes find their reason for being. It invades the campuses and even the high schools. Transcendental Meditation, most popular of the Eastern imports, is, in fact, part of the curriculum in a number of high schools, and this and other forms of meditation are taught in one form or another on scores of campuses. Reporting on this trend, historian Hal Bridges says in his recent book *American Mysticism* that "never before has the mystical strand been so discernible in American college and university life."

I think of individuals too. I think of a couple I know—the husband a Ph.D.—who took a year off from academic life to live alone in a one-room log hut on the edge of an icy river in the Arctic wilderness. I think of a young woman who spent a summer alone on a Florida key, "silent and growing." I remember a wandering student, picked up in Maine, who spent his nights sleeping under the stars, "trying to find out who I am and how I am like *other* living things."

More startling, if not more important, is the fact that meditation is also at the heart of a major change in the science laboratories and clinics of the country. Thinkers and experimenters from backgrounds as diversified as physics, psychology, psychiatry and general medicine are suddenly at work in what one can only call metaphysics, "the science of being"; looking, just as the great spiritual teachers have always looked, for the lost thread between mind and body; searching for potent and practical ways to use the one to help the other.

Exploring these experiments, we seem to be plunged at times into the labyrinths of science fiction. Is it possible that bona-fide physicists study psychokinesis—the ability of the mind to make an object move? That erudite and disciplined psychiatrists and psychologists experiment with psychic healing, seriously discuss the healing values of meditation and invite gurus into their laboratories to demonstrate the control of mind over body? It is possible; it is true.

Consider the following news stories culled from recent books, newspapers and magazines. At Wesleyan University in Middletown, Connecticut, a graduate student experimenting in the laboratory uses his brain to control his heart. He gets up to 142 beats a minute; he has lowered it to 42. In New York, at America's largest nursing school, the Division of Nurse Education of New York University, 130 graduate students are learning psychic healing with the "laying on of hands." In Minnesota, Stillwater State Prison studies the effects of Transcendental Meditation on the behavior, morale and rehabilitation of a group of inmates. And at the prestigious Institute of Living, in Hartford, TM is used to help mentally ill patients recover.

The general public has long been aware of the experimentation in parapsychology going on at Duke University; but it seems largely unaware that this new subject is also part of the curriculum of many other colleges. As of 1974, in fact, there were more than a hundred, and in 1969 the Parapsychological Association established its legitimacy by winning membership in the American Association for the Advancement of Science.

In New York, the Maimonides Medical Center has a division of Parapsychology and Psychophysics, and in the

Dream Laboratory of the same center "the image of a painting is transmitted by ESP and seems to enter the dreams of a laboratory subject sleeping in another room." Still other laboratories explore the effects of fear or kindness on plants, or investigate telepathy and clairvoyance.

Perhaps the most startling demonstration of the new interest occurred at the annual meeting of the American Psychiatric Association in the spring of 1974 in Detroit, where a panel sponsored by the Association's then newly appointed Task Force on Meditation featured "the interface between psychiatry and mysticism" and presented lectures and slides on various forms of psychic phenomena, including faith healing. The meeting drew a crowd of 650 lay and professional people, believed to be the largest attendance at any panel discussion in the Association's history.

Dr. Dean, who chaired the meeting, has coined the word "metapsychiatry," which, he tells us, is "a term born of necessity to indicate the relationship between psychiatry and mysticism," a relationship which until now the Association has surely spent little time contemplating. Dr. Dean has also written a paper (which, incidentally, has been read into *The Congressional Record*) in which he sets forth with respect and accuracy the phenomenon of the mystic experience.

Legions of other experiments pop up everywhere. At the Foundation for Mind Research, Masters and Houston work with their students to produce creative imagery through meditation or even through trance. In some laboratories, meditation itself is studied. Transcendental Meditation, in particular, has been the subject of innumerable laboratory studies, and it appears to be beyond doubt that, during the meditative process which TM teaches, the meditator's oxygen consumption decreases, indicating that the person is in a state of deep rest. Experimenters have also discovered that even outside their meditative periods the people who practice Transcendental Meditation are able to recover from stress more quickly than those who don't, that their reaction time is speeded up and that their motor performance and learning ability are increased.

As noted earlier, the Institute of Living, in Hartford, a sanitarium for the mentally ill, also uses the deep relaxation of this form of meditation to help its patients. The patient, to be sure, does not get *well* because he is meditating. But it helps. Matching his meditators with a control group, Dr. Bernard Glueck, Jr., director of research, found that with meditation there was a considerable reduction in the manifestations of anxiety. Their hands trembled less, they perspired less, and so forth. They also slept much better. In fact, most of them were able to give up sedation. With such deep rest possible, and with the layers of symptoms stripped away, therapists at the Institute found it easier to get at the root of the patients' problems, and many of the patients improved. Many of them also went on meditating after they had left the Institute!

Other laboratories study Kirlian photography, an exotic import from Russia. It is not really photography, says one of its foremost exponents in this country, nor do we know how it works. What happens is that a small amount of high-voltage, high-frequency current is introduced into the subject of the "picture," and the subsequent discharge is recorded on photographic film. Look at it on film as it was shown at the American Psychiatric Association meeting and you will see the shadowy picture of the object surrounded by what is sometimes called an "energy field" or a "bionic field," a kind of aura or halo which looks like the very coronas that sensitives have been claiming to see for centuries, like the extra, ethereal body which these people say we all have. The corona, as it appears in the Kirlian photographs, pales in some illnesses, brightens in the healthy, is blotched in the anxious, fiercely red for the intoxicated person, bunched like fists for the angry. With inanimate objects the glow is always the same; in people it changes with the changes of mood—in size, shape, intensity and color.

Still a mystery, research on its possibilities barely started, Kirlian photography already seems to confirm the interdependence of mind and body which is so much a part of the inward revolution, and it has aroused the interest of numerous psychologists and psychiatrists. Recently when I visited the Institute of Living and talked with Dr. Glueck, I found that, in addition to using Transcendental Meditation with a number of his patients, he is pondering the use of Kirlian photography as a diagnostic tool; and bright, coronaed Kirlian pictures ornament the walls at the entrance of his office.

Perhaps no experimentation on the intricate harmony of mind and body has zoomed as fast as biofeedback. Scarcely known before 1969, even among psychologists, let alone by the general public, it has swiftly become a vast storehouse of experimentation and knowledge, pouring through the headlines of magazines and newspapers and annually spawning scores of articles and books. It has its own society, and so startling were the findings presented at the first meeting of that society in 1969 that thousands of requests for transcripts of the meeting were received from biomedical scientists all over the world.

What is biofeedback? And what is its link with medita-

tion, with the contemporary longing to know and understand man's inner being?

The full answer to that question is far too complex to
be dealt with in so brief a space; but at one level, the
definition of biofeedback, it is fairly simple. Imagine that
you are trying to learn to play golf. You step up to the
tee, and, to your astonishment, your instructor blindfolds
you before you play. You protest indignantly and rightly.
How can you learn to play if you don't know where the
ball is going? What you need is *feedback—information*
about how you are doing, so that you can make the proper
adjustments.

Feedback is, in fact, a universal experience in our lives.
A very common example is the thermostat which "discovers" that the room is getting cold and feeds this information back to the furnace, which in turn acts accord-
ingly. There are feedback systems also in all living things
and certainly in our own bodies. We touch something unexpectedly hot, for example, and the information that it
is hot moves instantaneously to the brain, which, in turn,
instructs us to use our muscles to snatch the hand away.

Innumerable other instances come to mind. Every day,
every hour, we use *bio*feedback—the biological information we need to guide our behavior. But we have assumed
through all the centuries of the development of Western
science that we could use biofeedback to control only the
limited part of our body which we called the voluntary
system. We could instruct and thus control our hands,
our legs, our eyelids, our speech, but no one supposed that
we could tell our internal organs and glands, our muscle
cells and circulation and heart how to behave.

Now researchers in the laboratories are discovering with
great excitement that the mind and the will can control

nearly all body activities. "Biofeedback techniques," says Barbara Brown, "have been investigated as a therapeutic tool for everything from annoying jerky eye movements to incapacitating spastic muscle activity to learning control of artificial limbs, all with an encouraging degree of success." And she adds, "We now know that deep relaxation can vastly improve health and that with biofeedback techniques people can learn profound relaxation fairly rapidly."

Recently I tried a very simple version of biofeedback. In the display room at the American Psychiatric Association's annual meeting a group of people were demonstrating a fascinating device. Strapping a temperature-recording instrument on my wrist, the demonstrator suggested that I keep my eye on it and see if I could bring up the temperature of my hand. Though I had considerable theoretical knowledge of biofeedback, it was still astonishing to discover that even without willing it, simply by letting the suggestion lodge somewhere in my mind, it could happen. The temperature of my hand did rise three degrees in as many minutes.

In the more sophisticated laboratory experiments the process is a lot more complicated, but essentially the same. You sit comfortably in a chair and are wired to an instrument that records the rise and fall of whatever is being studied—skin resistance, heartbeat, blood pressure, brain waves or whatever. You try to bring about the desired result—increase your heartbeat, let's say, or relax muscle tension—and your success or failure is recorded on the instrument you are looking at, thus enabling you to tell how well you are doing. That's biofeedback; and scores of researchers are now working on it with a boundless enthusiasm matched only by the possibilities of this new linkage between body and mind.

An even more dramatic experiment in biofeedback is the monitoring of brain waves. Just as we can see, measure and control what is happening to hearts and muscles and temperature, so we can see, measure and control brain waves—the mysterious waves "which represent a continuous movement of electrical changes in the brain." In the laboratory, these waves are identifiable. There is beta, the kind of wave which seems to be present when we are getting our daily chores done; there is delta, which accompanies sleep; most important, there are alpha and theta. The alpha state is relaxed, pleasurable, restful, mind at ease; the theta often seems to resemble the state experienced by the person who is creating something or even by the mystic.

Again, to observe all this happening—and, in time, control it—the experimenter simply sits in a comfortable chair, with an electroencephalograph attached to his head to record the brain waves, and with a screen in front of him to see them. Already many thousands of Americans have tried the experiment. Most of them have been readily able to increase the pleasurable, relaxing alpha waves, and —in experimentation which is barely beginning, notably at Menninger—a growing number have been learning to increase their theta experience.

Biofeedback is not in itself meditation, though brain-wave biofeedback has been used since its inception as an aid to meditation; and the subjective phenomena reported in alpha biofeedback has many similarities to the phenomena reported in zen and yoga states. But biofeedback's greatest importance as a part of the architecture of the new landscape with which this book is concerned is its overwhelming proof of the power and energy of the mind and its as yet unexplored capacities.

This is a new dream, at least in the West, this dream of

harmony between mind and body; and it has led many doctors, psychiatrists and psychologists, by a kind of inexorable logic, to an exploration of psychic healing, that chancy, mysterious faculty which has so often been used by charlatans to gull the public. Is it possible that there is something in it, that the power of the mind really can cure a physical illness? Well, one can at least say that reputable scientists are experimenting with it; and in many phases of this healing change, meditation—the route to the deep mind, the true self—holds a central place. For example, Dr. Carl Simonton, who was, for a while, chief of radiation therapy at Travis Air Force Base in California, tried the experiment of instructing patients who came to him for cobalt therapy to "meditate" on their cancers, visualizing the growth crumbling away under the assault of the cobalt, visualizing "an army of millions of tiny white blood cells attacking the cancer cells and carrying them off." He found, without much surprise, that the patients who gave real attention to this mental assault responded better to radiation therapy than those who did not.

Other doctors and psychiatrists, fascinated with the steadily growing proof of the power of mind over body, study the so-called faith healer. What is it he is doing for the patient? What is passing between them? Why does he sometimes fail, and sometimes apparently succeed? If he is using the power of mind over body, how is he using it?

Perhaps the most exhaustive such study has been done by New York psychologist Lawrence LeShan. LeShan assembled a list of individuals who could be called "serious psychic healers" and spent five years studying them and reading what they had written about their healing powers. Then he took the logical step of trying it for himself. If he put in practice all that he had learned, could he too heal the sick? After a year and a half of experimentation and practice he found that he could indeed.

Not always, of course; not even often. Psychic healers, like doctors, cannot cure all of their patients; and, contrary to general opinion, most such cures are not instantaneous, though some are, as Dr. LeShan found to his astonishment.

Impressed by this newfound ability, Dr. LeShan during the last four years has trained more than 150 would-be healers to do the same thing. LeShan believes that the patient's self-healing mechanisms are mobilized by the healer, and, as we shall see in this and the next chapter, meditation, which makes it possible for patient and healer to be "merged" with each other, plays a large part in the healing process.

"None of us," Dr. LeShan theorizes, "do anything as well as we potentially can. We can all learn to read faster, jump higher, discriminate colors more precisely, reason more accurately, and so on through practically any abilities you can name. One of these abilities is the ability to heal ourselves, our ability of self-repair and self-recuperation. This too usually operates far below potential."

But Dr. LeShan believes that the ability to mobilize the patient's resources is possible only through caring— a prayerful, loving caring. For a moment, he says, the healer knows that "All Is One." This "knowledge" is somehow transmitted to the patient, who is then "back at home in the universe," is no longer "cut off," is living the full life of the "amphibian" in both land and water; and this return to the universe is itself healing.

Dr. LeShan illustrates that with the story of an elderly

woman who came to him for help because she had a very painful arthritis and swelling in her hands. She could hold and use a pencil or a knife and fork but with difficulty because she could not bring her fingers closer than one inch from her palm. Even trying brought severe pain. Her family had persuaded her to come to Dr. LeShan, though she herself had no belief in the possibility of psychic healing. Dr. LeShan ignored this and suggested that she read a newspaper while he was working; and she did. As for LeShan himself, he sought to go into the altered state of consciousness he calls Clairvoyant Reality—a profound in-depth perception in which what one sees is not individual objects or persons but the relationship of all things, the wholeness of the universe, the unity of all people. In this altered state of consciousness, he was able to feel that he and his patient were one, that they had merged. After he had sat thus for a while he passed his hands over her crippled left hand.

Five minutes later it was over. They chatted for a while and she said she had felt nothing unusual. "Then," says Dr. LeShan, "I asked the other members of her family to come back in (they had gone into the next room when I started the healing). Her husband asked her if there had been any effect. She replied, 'No. It's the same as it was,' and, to demonstrate this, flapped the fingers of both hands. To everyone's surprise—certainly including hers and mine—they swung easily to the palm and out again." She now, he added, "had full and painless movement of the fingers" and still had it a year later.

What is going on here? Dr. LeShan feels that "the healer sets up a situation which sometimes mobilizes the patient's self-repair mechanisms and the patient heals himself."

In time we may indeed come to realize that no magic is operating here but rather a perfectly normal physiological process whose skills we have allowed ourselves to forget. Not long ago, while I was in the Midwest traveling and interviewing for this book, I caught a cold that dipped suddenly into laryngitis, and my voice was reduced to a whisper. This problem might not have mattered except that only two days later I was due to lead a seminar at a retreat in the Carolina mountains, a task which would certainly involve at least six or seven hours of pretty continuous talking.

I tried conventional medicines, but they didn't seem to help. So, in despair and without much belief that it would accomplish anything, I tried deep meditation, repeating—silently, perforce!—a mantra of my own devising.

I was still saying it when, in the bitter cold of an early-spring morning in Michigan, I caught a six-o'clock plane. My seminar was now only twenty-four hours away, and still I couldn't speak above a whisper. It occurred to me that anyone with any sense would have turned around and gone home; but the seminar was scheduled and it was too late for a substitute. Besides, I could not shake the conviction that it was going to be all right.

If so, there was no sign of it when, to the horror of my hosts, I went to bed that night still not talking. Nevertheless, I stubbornly continued the inner discipline, which, if it did nothing else, felt so quieting, so healing; and I was really not much surprised when at nine the next morning the voice was back, scarcely even hoarse and entirely adequate for six hours of talking.

Once upon a time I'd have thought—as you might—miracle! But I now saw it simply for what I think it was: a marshaling of the body's own resources, a way of using self-healing processes that, as every doctor knows, are a part of everyone's arsenal.

After all, that is not as surprising as it appears at first sight. We've been conditioned for years to the knowledge that our minds can make us ill. Which of us has not been told by a doctor that what we are suffering from is anxieties and tensions—that if we will only relax, our ulcers will improve, our spastic colons calm down, our headaches grow fewer? We are all used to that; but how can you believe in psychosomatic illness without believing also in psychosomatic health? At Menninger, the Greens, experimenting in biofeedback and other mind-over-body techniques, point out that "if we can make ourselves ill, then we must also be able to make ourselves well."

Mind over body, mind with body—it is a new-old dream coming to fruition as the inward revolution leads the way. The deep mind can heal the body; it can be a listening post from which to hear the signals of health, good and bad; and it can supply a lifetime of preventive medicine. Recently support for this came from a dramatic source—a newspaper report on the people of the famous Hunza Valley, which is up in the tricorner where Afghanistan, Tibet and the Soviet Union meet. These people are celebrated for their long lives—many live past the century mark—and for their vigor, which often lets them work hard, marry, and have children at an age when most Westerners, if alive at all, are in the tottering stage. They live on a simple diet, primarily apricots and whole grains. But recently it has also been discovered that they do something else. Beginning when they are children they practice profound relaxation several times a day all their lives. People who have been there say it is not unusual to see children and adults drop what they are doing, sit down anywhere, even on the ground, fall into deep relaxation which may last ten or fifteen minutes, and then, refreshed, go on with their labor.

The capacity to heal is one of the most controversial of the gifts of meditation but also one of the most significant, since it declares the reality of the alliance of mind and body, the intricate and sensitive interplay of cell and muscle, heart and breath with the inner self which powers our lives. Suddenly face to face with the capacities of the human psyche, members of the healing professions—like many other people involved in the inward revolution—are seeing their world change overnight and, slowly but surely, are beginning to use this change in ways that must in time benefit all of us.

CHAPTER 5

How Long Will It Last?

Turning inward—often, initially, out of despair and hopelessness—a generation unexpectedly finds itself in the midst of major discovery. But a serious question remains: Will the new movement last long enough to make the changes in our world that these discoveries foreshadow?

In our swiftly changing era, movements come and go, enthusiasms sweep over the continent like wind in a wheat field and vanish. Is this what will happen now? Are we in the midst of a passing fad which will blow itself out? Some critics think so; they find signs of transiency in the very fever of the movement. Others argue that it is an escapist mood which will vanish when we feel more able to cope or when something else takes our attention. "This sitting around meditating is just another mood." The speaker was a lawyer, a participant in a living-room dialogue based on a discussion of changes in the seventies. "It will pass the way the riots on the campus passed."

Is it true? Well, of course, it could be. Historic movements *are* in part transitory; and there *are* retreats as well as advances in everything. This era closes, that opens, and people do get weary of their enthusiasms. And, of course, the movement has its share of cranks, kooks and hustlers who from time to time will be exposed and toppled. Charlatans too abound; so do people with an eager eye on the dollar; so do the naïve, the born followers, the people who will try anything new. One is sometimes reminded of the comment of a character in the movie *Separate Tables*. "The trouble with being on the side of right," he said gloomily, "is the company you keep."

Then, too, meditation, properly carried out, is not easy, and its intent can be frightening. It forces us to confront ourselves and our predicaments, and to face the challenges of our unused potential. Nonetheless, when I listen to these critics I am convinced that they have little notion of the magnitude of what is going on. Concentrating on the faddists and charlatans, they ignore the profound meaning of the movement and miss an understanding of contemporary history.

True, the fanfare over meditation will, no doubt, die down and its more bizarre elements grow less popular. Time may winnow the followers, the headlines may shift to new interests; but what serious people sought and found in this major change in our thinking is not likely to be lost.

Even now the evaluations grow more sober, the original flippancy with which most of us as journalists greeted the movement has nearly vanished, and hundreds of serious books, monographs and doctoral theses have been written about it. "We are well out of the phase of the Crazies and well into the phase of the Artists," points out William Irwin Thompson in his book *Passages about Earth*.

The flippancy is vanishing; and there are reasons—

good, sound reasons—for expecting that the quiet revolution is here to stay. For one thing, we are discovering that it is not a kind of air pocket in the water pipe, a detour, an unrelated moment in the midst of an otherwise self-satisfied and materialistic century. Far from being a disconnection with the rapidly changing technological decades that preceded it, it is the child of those decades, born out of their anguish. In particular it is a natural extension of the tumultuous sixties. Perhaps *that* was a decade we didn't understand very well! At any rate it is too much to say, as my lawyer friend did, that the riots on the campus were a mood; nor have they passed. Though students are no longer taking over the dean's office, and though cameras have gone back to snapping graduation-day pictures instead of pictures of armed blacks "liberating" buildings, the bullets of Kent State still burn the air of America, and the memory of what the young were doing and saying is written not only in the history books but in the earthquake-shocked minds of millions of Americans.

As I write this, it is ten years since the student rebellion of the sixties started with a bang on the Berkeley campus of the University of California. Though its roots probably went far deeper, it began—in the public view at least—when the college closed off part of a campus area where the students had been allowed to agitate for off-campus political or social-action causes. As a result, a wide spectrum of students belonging to all political persuasions came together swiftly to form a united front called the Free Speech Movement, which demanded that students be free from university regulation of their political activity. Helped on by eloquent orators among the students and fanned by the fires of Vietnam, the movement swept through other campuses and became a multifaceted crusade, often violent, which was intended to change America at the root.

I traveled a great deal during those years, and I remember the inflammatory leaflets passed out at the gates of Columbia University, the raging young blacks in Harlem, the impassioned marches through the streets of Washington, and the young man preparing to participate in one of those marches who told me, "In my lifetime we're going to tear it all down—the whole crummy hypocritical structure—and make America good again."

The violence was there, all right; and it was real. But the mood of inwardness, the spiritual longing—though far less visible in the era of the secular city—was growing right along with it; growing out of it would be a better way to say it. I remember a night in New Haven, Connecticut, in 1965. Bishop James Pike was in the midst of defending his widely publicized theological "heresies" and had come to speak to the Yale students. A large auditorium had been assigned, but it was plain almost at once that even standing room would not accommodate the crowds. A bigger one was hastily found; and I have never forgotten the river of young men—hundreds and hundreds of young men—who rushed out into the streets of the city, disdaining the sidewalks, jostling and trying to outrun one another in the effort to get a front seat to hear a bishop of the Episcopal Church speak on theology. When we were finally, breathlessly, seated, I asked the student next to me why this remarkable performance.

"Because what he's saying is something we care about a lot," he said. "People think we aren't religious. Well, we are. We just want to cut out the crap and get to what religion is all about."

I saw it again in 1968 in Uppsala, Sweden, where I was

attending a meeting of the World Council of Churches. As church meetings go it was a very activist one indeed, concerned with the problems of the Third World, with hunger and disease and injustice. To the young delegates and observers, however, it scarcely moved at all in these directions, and they picketed and protested at every turn. What is even more interesting, however, in the light of the turn to inwardness which was so soon to be visible, is that they protested as strongly about a lack of spirituality, and held their own worship services. One night, for example, they fasted and prayed all night in the thousand-year-old cathedral.

On another night, near the end of the sessions, the two movements came into exact juxtaposition. It was nearly midnight at the end of a long, exhausting day, and I, for one, desperately wanted to go home and to bed; but the kids were forming a parade, carrying violent anti–Vietnam war banners, and apparently ready to take some sort of action. So, remembering that I was there as a reporter, I fell in line behind them, convinced that the peace of the city was about to be disturbed somewhere. I followed them for miles across the ancient town, and in due time we arrived, not at the barricades but at the Church of the Covenant, Uppsala's oldest church. Inside there were no demonstrations, only a long and sorrowful service, a steady lament—with song, speech from the pews, drumbeat—of the sins of their world.

At two o'clock, as the early Swedish dawn began to shine through the leaves outside the windows of the ancient church, they ended the service, saying the Lord's Prayer together in the languages of more than sixty countries.

Looking back over the decade, it seems to me that the

violence was like the bursting from the earth of springs whose deep source was still to be made clear. At any rate, by the end of the sixties the passionate devotion of the kids to the ethic of social action was really beginning to change, outwardly at least. Since 1970 I've been traveling again, listening to the students, who, instead of rioting, talk about the Light, the Knowledge, meditation, body training, communication, Jesus and Buddha. In many ways they seem altogether different from their predecessors; but you cannot talk with them at all without finding that their cry is still "We have to change the world."

The truth is that the activism of the last decade was the symptom rather than the disease; a symptom of profound dissatisfaction with the society. The dissatisfaction remains—intensified by recent political and economic events. "Worry over political morality," declared Gallup after a 1974 study, "is replacing anger over the Vietnam war."

The dissatisfaction remains; and just as the stream of spiritual longing ran under the tempestuous activism of the sixties, so, conversely, a quieter but as real activism runs below—and is related to—the new spiritual longing. I myself find no "pond of calm and contentment"; nor did Gallup's survey. "Although the mood on college campuses today is calmer than in the turbulent sixties," he wrote, "there is little evidence to suggest that the current college scene is as serene as it was in the 1950's." Nearly four in ten college students, he reported, "continue to believe that violence is sometimes justified to bring about a change in society"; and he added that "college students today also differ sharply from students of the Fifties in their dedication to bringing about societal change by becoming involved in the 'helping' professions, such as teaching and social work. Gallup surveys have shown that more than half of college students have at some point worked among poor and underprivileged groups."

We are still dissatisfied; but now—perhaps partly out of despair—the dissatisfaction expresses itself differently. Whereas formerly young people wanted to set the world right by changing institutions, now they want to set it right by changing people.

But the passion of the demand has not altered. What we are dealing with has been called "a fundamental neurosis"—a sense of having failed in our relationships with one another, with God, and with our own inward selves; and, as with most neuroses, it will burden us until we find some way to change it.

This is the *first* of the reasons why to say that we are in the midst of a passing fad is a gigantic misnomer; but a *second* reason to expect some degree of permanence is that meditation, after all, is a normal part of life, a part of life which is as much intended for our use as our eyes are or our ears or our hands. What is abnormal is not the search for the Self that is now going on, but the near-obliteration of that search in the sterile generations through which we have just passed.

A *third* reason for the expectation of permanence is that, as noted in an earlier chapter, this change in our outlook is a response to our need to find more flexible and imaginative ways of *living and working in our swiftly changing society.* With the sharpened vision that has grown out of a disordered century, we see the bewildering variety of routes into the future, see them perhaps more consciously than people ever did before, and understand—as perhaps also no one ever did before—our staggering need for wisdom. "We'll have to start over again from within ourselves," warned a young law student as we sat together recently on a train, peering out murky windows at passing slums and visibly polluted air.

We will indeed. But rethinking values, changing conceptions of reality, making ourselves over, is the hardest thing we can do. It takes enormous wisdom, tolerance and understanding to scrap old values and find new ones; to relate facts, ideas and experiences to each other in new ways; to find out how to change our world and change it before it is too late. And whom have we to turn to for wisdom to shape these new values except other human beings like ourselves? And where can they—and we—find that extra wisdom except in the profound and knowledgeable resources in our inner selves?

A *fourth* reason for anticipating permanence is that the longer we stay with this movement, the more likelihood there is that it will become part of our lives, since it is uniquely qualified to set in motion forces which cannot be turned back. One is reminded of the body of knowledge which accumulated with such dazzling speed during the Industrial Revolution.

This, of course, is particularly true in the science laboratory. In the previous chapter we examined at length the involvement of scientists both natural and behavioral in the new movement. Since the writing of that chapter, reports of still more experiments, more research, more recruits, more theses, more organizations, have deluged my desk. For example—to pick only a few—*Saturday Review* devoted an issue to what it called "the expansion of the limits of consciousness"; Dr. Dean of the American Psychiatric Association's Task Force on Meditation is editing an anthology called *Psychiatry and Mysticism* which is a summary by many contributors of what is being done to harmonize these so recently divergent fields; Menninger's is in the midst of an ambitious program of alpha and theta training for college students; at Wainwright House in Rye, New York, Jean Houston, in 1974, did a twenty-day program of continuous seminars and workshops "to reopen dormant mental, physical and emotional capacities"; in Canada two professors of the psychology of religion—Jesuit scholars both—are teaching an extension course at the University of Ottawa entitled "Breakthrough in Human Potential," a journey into psychic phenomena which has drawn the largest enrollment of any extension course ever offered at that university.

In the summer of 1975, the Second International Congress on Psychotronic Research has been held in Monte Carlo, Monaco. "Psychotronics"—a word which most of us have never heard of—is defined as the scientific investigation of the interactions among consciousness, energy and matter. In 1974 an extensive eight-week advanced training program was offered at the distinguished Tibetan Buddhist center of Nyingma in California—offered primarily for psychologists and mental-health professionals; and the same center established, on the New York–Connecticut border, a project for applying Tibetan Buddhist psychology and meditative practice to mental disorder. One could go on and on. In an unforgettable metaphor, Arthur Koestler declared that modern scientists are "Peeping Toms at the keyholes of eternity."

All this has been a shock to behavioral scientists in particular, and many, of course, are aghast. But the expressed shock of these critics has not halted the continuing experiments, and it does not seem likely to in the future. In fact, in England, a poll taken among the readers of *The New Scientist*, a magazine that goes mostly to scientists and technicians, came up with startling results: nearly 70 percent said they believed in the possibility of extrasensory perception!

The result of all this endorsement is that today people are less afraid of the unconscious, less afraid of altered states of consciousness, less afraid of admitting to inward experience of their own. Since I began this book, I've made a habit of sitting down by strangers in trains and planes and at social gatherings and, as soon as possible, casually introducing the word "meditation" into the conversation. Almost without exception, it is met with responses like "Oh, I've just spent a weekend at Dialogue House in New York," or "I've just finished reading a book on Transcendental Meditation," or "Last summer I went to a retreat sponsored by my church. There was a lot of meditation, and some faith healing too." In fact, the populace is seeded with hordes of people who have had experience with meditative techniques and related forms of mind expansion. Millions of Americans have been involved in this new phenomenon in ways that have changed many of them very deeply.

By now, hosts of volunteers who have discovered that they can relax their tired muscles, get rid of their migraines, lower their blood pressure, are equipped with something they're not likely to forget. So are those who have had profound experiences of self-knowledge, loving communication with others, feelings of unity with their world and their God.

Moreover, a very special kind of cumulative confirmation comes from the belated discovery by the scientific community that mystics and people interested in altered states of consciousness are not necessarily muddleheaded, credulous or psychotic, but rather that they number among their ranks some of the foremost thinkers of the past and of our own time, a totally sane group of open-minded, serious and often profound people. It was this discovery that so dumbfounded Dr. Dean in the early days of his researches. He was impressed, he said, "to find that great numbers of sensible, rational people in all walks of life, lay and professional, believed in the ultraconscious, had themselves experienced various manifestations of it, and had derived constructive benefits from it."

For the first time a modern, industrialized, articulate society has had a multiple exposure to these experiencing individuals and to the phenomena that interests them; and one of the most interesting results is that the new adventures in consciousness have ceased to be the sacrosanct property of the young. Everywhere, fascinated older people try meditative techniques and spiritual journeys of all kinds. The kids are opening doors, but so also are their elders. Here is an electrical engineer building his own bio-feedback equipment; a computer programmer learning healing therapies; a lawyer trying to explain meditation techniques at a luncheon meeting of his colleagues; a doctor faithfully attending healing sessions of the Spiritual Frontiers Fellowship; and a priest psychologist at Yale Divinity School leaving to spend his sabbatical year with the Trappists as a full participant "in a discipline of silence and hard physical labor."

The *fifth* reason why we will not easily be rid of what is happening to us is the tremendous *cross culture* caused by our mobility and our ease of communication. Through the peripatetic media, through travel and through common need, people of all sorts and of all areas of the world pass in and out of one another's lives as easily as moisture flows from the air into the ocean and back again into the clouds and so again into the sea. This is especially true of the liberal community of exploring and caring people who have a growing longing for new styles of life. All across the world, they find and recognize one another.

A letter comes in my mail from a self-taught scholar in India who wants to know more about meditative practices in America; an acquaintance returns from a trip to the Antarctic having encountered on the ship a Spaniard who shared her feelings about the painter Kandinsky; a woman I met in England a year ago told me that she was corresponding with a young American who was taking a sabbatical year at a monastery in Thailand.

Disregarding not only geographic distance but every other boundary line as well, the physicist joins forces with the philosopher and the psychologist; the priest and the artist find common cause. Christians and Jews share their concern for a world of love and justice; Christians and Buddhists share spiritual longing; Christians and Communists hold dialogues with each other; scientists and clergymen share their understanding of reality. In place of the celebrated generation gap, bridges of all kinds are spanning gulfs between exploratory young people and spiritually mobile adults.

As for the young themselves, kids from different nations know each other far better than young people from neighboring towns did when I was a teen-ager. You see them sitting together, the wandering young of all countries, in the malls and squares of the cities of the world; in Copenhagen and London; in Istanbul and Rome; in Montreal and Mexico. They find each other; and so do their elders. Dr. Dean himself acquired his first interest in the world of metapsychiatry when he went to Tokyo as a tourist and chanced to see the filming of Zen Buddhist rituals. Now, Dr. Jean Houston told me with great enthusiasm, "We have East and West; we have a global village; we have wise men and shamans and technicians and crazies and cults all meeting and talking to one another. We have a remarkable meshing of the tapestry of the world, a meshing which is necessary for this movement to take hold and last."

The *final* reason why the discoveries of the seventies aren't likely to melt away like snow in April is that there are serious people who believe that these discoveries constitute a gigantic leap up the evolutionary staircase. At the very least, the leaders of this movement think, with Harvey Cox, that we are "witnessing the overture to a sweeping cultural renaissance, a revolution of human sensibilities in which the faculties we have starved and repressed during the centuries of industrialization will be nourished and appreciated again." At the most, they think mankind may be taking a great evolutionary step toward a fast-coming day when we will use faculties of consciousness whose very presence in ourselves we have barely acknowledged. They speak persuasively of an "adventure in consciousness," "an evolutionary development of the human nervous system," "the emergence of a new human nature," and they believe that spiritual geniuses are as they are because they have taken an evolutionary leap ahead of the rest of us and stand already on a plateau toward which we should all be struggling.

Such people naturally reject the notion that they form part of a conservative, escapist movement and, instead, regard themselves as the vanguard of a radical one, the vanguard of a movement comparable to that of our remote ancestors who came out of the cave and the forest into the fertile fields. "It is my thesis," declares George Leonard in his book *The Transformation,* "that the current period is indeed unique in history and that it represents the beginning of the most thorough-going change in the quality of human existence since the creation of an agricultural surplus brought about the birth of civilized states some five thousand years ago."

"We think of ourselves as seizing the evolution," Dr. Masters told me as we moved about among the tools and artifacts of past and future which fill his extraordinary house. There are many who agree—who believe that, for the first time in man's fumbling progress, human beings are able to influence the speed of evolution, to make the next stage come faster.

True, views like these did not spring up for the first time in the seventies. Indeed, the idea was propounded years ago by Dr. Richard Maurice Bucke, a remarkable man who, far in advance of his time, was at once a psychiatrist and a mystic. Dr. Bucke believed that "a seemingly miraculous higher consciousness" that has kept appearing among spiritual geniuses throughout history is latent in all of us as an evolutionary process, and that the human race is destined to continue evolving from self-consciousness to the cosmic consciousness that great religious leaders like Buddha, Jesus Christ and Mohammed have already attained. In more recent times this strikes an echo again in the writings of Teilhard de Chardin, who passionately believed that "evolution is an ascent toward consciousness."

For people who have convictions like these, meditation —whether through its capacity to develop imagery or through the ways in which it can take one to the juncture point of time and eternity—is one of the prime routes of an accelerated evolution.

The era of inwardness has only begun. Its first overt signs were written on the tablets of change by the mid-sixties; but there is no reason to believe that it will somehow go away. On the contrary, its presence at the heart of America is changing all our lives. It has changed the preoccupations of researchers in behavioral-science laboratories to an unprecedented degree. In fact, some behavioral scientists are even beginning to replace the term "unconscious" with the much more spiritually weighted term "psyche."

It has altered individuals—many individuals—enough so that they are a yeasty leaven in the world of our time. It is unquestionably changing, or at least paralleling, a new consciousness in the world of art. The soul, the deep unconscious, looks out of a myriad of contemporary paintings, rendering them mysterious and incomprehensible to many older Americans who grew up in a more literal world. Music, too, often deliberately makes itself a forcing ground for developing "soul." In the wake of rock music's effort to change everyday perceptions, serious people are producing tapes and records intended to induce altered states of consciousness, and are setting up workshops and conferences to study ways of using music to enhance imagery.

Inevitably, churches too are beginning to feel the effect of change. Seemingly overnight, millions of people are embarked again on the search for God. True, many of them never enter a church door. The singing, testifying young are in the streets, not in the pews; and so, often, are their exploring elders.

Still, the churches are currently seeded by numerous groups which though not always *of* the church are technically within it. One thinks of the charismatic Pentecostal groups with their emphasis on the Holy Spirit, their ecstatic, spontaneous prayer or song or even speaking with tongues; of the Spiritual Frontiers Fellowship; of Camps

Farthest Out, the retreat movement "where it is as natural to talk about the things of the Spirit as it is to talk about the daily news." Though somewhat alien, these movements nonetheless run within the church like a stream of brilliant light through the pews; or, better, they are within it as a sprouting seed is in the soil.

And there *are* signs of rebirth, of return to the roots, in the church proper. After all, the new movement, with its staircase of exploration from personal identity to love, to the experience of God, is indigenous to the church in a very special way. In her book *Contemplating Now*, Monica Furlong writes: "Most religious traditions have struggled with the idea that God is a part of, or is within or *is* the individual human psyche."

So they have; but, caught in the midst of a scientific, secular world—a needy world, moreover, that seemed to require concrete action—the churches in the Sixties began to act as though their slogan was "If you can't beat them, join them." Almost overnight the very words "spirit" and "soul" became anathema; and men and women were adjured to forget their fascination with metaphysical worlds and attend to the needs of this one.

In 1967, I did a major survey among Protestant ministers, asking their opinions about a number of the religious directions of the time. I found a sizable minority, perhaps a third, who said, in one way or another, that God language was taboo. It was time to act, they said, not to sit about nursing one's own soul.

But an explosion outside the church is now battering on its doors; and, in a startling irony, the science laboratories, which in a very real way banished the soul and removed religion from the center of men's lives, are now calling the church back to its traditional faith. We see the first beginnings of the return in experimental worship which stresses a transcendent God; in the return of the old-fashioned prayer meeting; in the setting up of many new retreat centers; in the faith healing which many main-line churches are now trying; perhaps most of all, in the life style of church task forces—groups which work hard on slum tutorials or halfway houses or racial problems or the rehabilitation of alcoholics, and still make time for daily periods of meditation.

Some of this certainly springs from a new kind of desire to be "with it." But this is changing, too, and the concern with transcendence is steadily growing and deepening.

Moreover, a minority of creative people, aided and abetted by the young, are beginning to rethink the Christian heritage. In January, 1975, an ecumenical group of distinguished Protestant, Roman Catholic and Orthodox thinkers met in a weekend conference at the Hartford Seminary Foundation and emerged with what may well be an historic document, a thesis they called "An Appeal for Theological Affirmation." The appeal pleaded for a retreat from secular attitudes and behavior, and for a return toward emphasis on God as a transcendental reality. The document pointed out that much of the church has lost touch with transcendence and that transcendence is, in effect, what Christianity is all about. The seminary, now in a process of reorganization, says it has many requests from churchmen for an opportunity to take special study in spiritual growth.

These new currents in the church have undoubtedly contributed to a rather startling Gallup report on the impact of the church. In 1970, says Gallup, 75 percent of the people thought the church's impact was becoming weaker; in 1975 only 56 percent thought that. In 1970, 14 percent thought religion was gaining ground; by 1975 it had soared to 31 percent. Some commentators indeed see not only a greatly increased spiritual affirmation in the church, but the creation of a lay theology, an effort by the man in the pew—and sometimes the man on the street—to translate into language the spiritual events that are happening in his own inner self.

As for education, the campus has been taken over with considerable speed. As we have already noted, innumerable colleges and universities offer courses in the whole paranormal field from extrasensory perception to meditation, and doctoral theses are written on such subjects as psychic healing, ESP and so forth. Visiting lecturers include researchers in biofeedback, altered states of consciousness, Kirlian photography and the like.

The mood too is different. On the once riot-torn Berkeley campus, young people now congregate at the Transcendental Meditation building. The Indian sitar plays on campuses at evening concerts; "soul" and "spirit" are usable words again; religion—of a sort—is far more welcome than it was. Indeed, enclaves of students interested in these matters on campus tend to occupy the same position as the small groups of political liberals several decades ago —out in front, interested and interesting.

Moreover, new colleges start up which actually focus around meditation—most notably the Maharishi International University, which has taken over the grounds of the bankrupt Parsons College in Iowa. Everyone on campus meditates, and it is to become a university in which the student takes two months of academic study and then one month of meditative practice and so forth, thus assuring himself that if he goes as far as a doctorate he will have spent two years in meditation.

Until recently, public schools barely caught the fringe of all this, with Transcendental Meditation appearing in a classroom or a school system here and there. Now, however, classrooms have been invaded by a whole range of experiments. Books and doctoral theses pop up everywhere, all intended to guide children into the new world of expanding consciousness. I came across one book called *Meditation for Little People,* and there is a Ph.D. candidate who is working out a program on the "transpersonal" nature of children, using writers like Blake and Hesse and books like Saint-Exupéry's *The Little Prince.* He is attempting also to document the paranormal experiences of children—experiences which are believed to be numerous, but which we habitually discourage.

Some schoolteachers are experimenting with taking their students on imaginary journeys relating to the subjects they are studying. For example, one high-school shop teacher tried relaxing his class through meditation and then had them imagine they were electrons being pulled and pushed by the fields around the induction coils! It worked, too. He claims he found the lesson much easier to teach.

The new inwardness shows up in innumerable other ways too. Joining forces with ecology, it teaches awareness of a living world whose fate is bound up with our own; and its effect on the drug culture has been startling. Thousands of youngsters have given up hard drugs and chosen instead to sit in silence at the feet of some teacher of meditation.

Altered states of consciousness are also being tried to change the mental state of ex-convicts. In Tulsa, Oklahoma, under the direction of Dr. Joseph Spears, who is the president and medical director of Tulsa's Rehabilitation, Research and Evaluation Program, forty-nine young men and women who had just been released from prison and tagged as borderline—meaning that they were likely to

go back—were given training in altered states of consciousness with the hope that they would understand themselves
better. That was in 1971. As of 1975, only two of these
young men and women have returned to prison, and one
has absconded. The rest apparently found in the inner
consciousness something that helped them solve their
problems. They were able to bring this to the surface and
thus change their lives.

But perhaps the most startling experiment is the one
just initiated by the Maharishi European Research University. Dr. Candace Borland of that university and her
research associate, Garland Landruth of Maharishi International University in Iowa, found themselves intrigued
by the Maharishi's conviction that if he could teach one
percent of the world's people to practice meditation, he
could change the world. So they have begun researching
what happens in cities where, in fact, one percent of people *are* enrolled in Transcendental Meditation.

In their study they matched twelve such cities with control cities, and their first and, so far, only completed experiment focused on crime. They found, so they say, that
in the "one percent" cities the crime rate decreased between 1972 and 1973 by an average of 8.08 percent, while
in the control cities the crime rate continued the melan-
choly rise we were accustomed to, at a rate of 7.8 percent
per year!

The figures seem unbelievable, and skepticism is justi-
fiable. But, on the other hand, it is part of our illness that
we no longer believe in the yeast of the individual, in
the astonishing power of the changed person.

Change *is* happening; and change begun in this field, as
in any other, has a certain irreversible quality. Like Adam
and Pandora we can't put knowledge back again on its

tree or in its box. Embedded in our lives now as the roots of grass are embedded in a good lawn, the inward movement is likely to survive all but the most devastating attack, the more so because there are now so many serious and disciplined people who will passionately struggle to keep it alive. In fact, explosions of new knowledge—and this is no less than that—never leave the world as it was before they happened. We are still feeling the effects of the Golden Age of Greece, the Reformation, the discovery of printing, the scientific explosion.

Will the inward revolution come to an end? All the signs and portents say it will not. Now the question is: how wide is the door that leads to these experiences and how far will it open for all of us?

CHAPTER 6

Learning to Meditate

~~~~~~

Can meditation be learned? Of course it can. It is not restricted to monks and saints and ascetics. It is the birthright of all of us and it has been learned, taught and self-taught all through history.

True, there is something disturbing about the very idea of being "taught" meditation. Some people are troubled by the use of techniques to invoke this most spontaneous —and most profound—part of one's self. There seems to be something dogged and purposeful about dealing this way with our essential creativity, with the most spiritual part of our lives. Moreover, though such learning is as ancient as time, it is a new lesson for Americans in the twentieth century, and the way into it seems prickly, difficult and faintly ridiculous. What's all this about flowers and incense and candle flames and mantras and sitting cross-legged and chanting? Why can't we just sit down and meditate?

There is a straightforward, simple answer which you can easily test for yourself. Stop what you are doing; sit down on the nearest chair and try to quiet your conscious mind, that noise-making obstacle which stands between you and the luminous quiet of inner space. How long, how well, can you hold off racing questions like "How am I going to finish my work on time? Where will I get the money to pay that bill? What's going to happen to my kids if they don't shape up? Will I get that job—or are they going to give it to that clown who doesn't begin to know as much about it as I do?" Even trying it is a revelation to most of us about what we are normally doing with our minds and about how hard it is to stop doing it. "The mind is like a mad monkey stung by a scorpion," said the great nineteenth-century Indian sage Ramakrishna.

So it is; and even more so today than it was in his more peaceful world. Like Stephen Leacock's celebrated horseman, tension-ridden twentieth-century Americans ride off in all directions at once and end up milling about in the center of the road. We are too nervous to be still. But it is stillness that is the latch on the gate that leads to the limitless kingdom of the Self. We must calm the waters if we are to see the bottom of the lake; we must end the busy talk if we are to listen to the musician.

Techniques of meditation are *primarily ways to help us do that.* Centuries of experience have proven that we cannot get rid of the clamoring, conscious mind by simply wishing it away; proven, too, that it is easier to concentrate if you are sitting on a straight-backed chair than in a comfortable lounger; easier to still the conscious mind and take its attention from its wounds and distractions if you give yourself something to center on.

Charles C. Wise, Jr., department counsel in the office of the Secretary of Defense, offers an apt illustration from the Army. "A mule-skinner," he says, "teaching army recruits how to train mules began by batting the mule between the eyes with a two-by-four. That is because 'the first and most important thing is to get the mule's attention.'" He adds that it is so with us. "Meditation," he says, "<u>begins when something captures our attention.</u> We invest interest and time in it; we care enough to desire to know more. Attention is the mind's attitude of devotion."

Agreeing, teachers of meditation from time immemorial have experimented with ways of quieting the conscious mind, cleansing and opening the doors of perception. Many of these ways are very ancient indeed. In Eastern countries they may go back unchanged for thousands of years. Indian monks and sages sat in lotus position, eyes on a mandala, long before the birth of Christ; and it should not be surprising that many of the techniques they have had time to perfect are elaborate and esoteric, and also pregnant with learned wisdom.

We too, here in America, to be sure, have a monastic tradition, a tradition of asceticism, discipline, prayer and aids to silence. But Western techniques are younger, simpler, and for the most part have been attached to organized religion, to a deliberate seeking for God. They may also begin with reflection and dialogue, with a dwelling on a certain idea; and on the whole these disciplines have been less diffused in the populace, less known by the public, than has been true in the East.

Traditional methods both East and West are very much with us right now—from the ancient Eastern ones to the Christian traditions of the West. And they take a prominent part in the whole inward movement. But, as we shall see later in the chapter, we are also rapidly inventing contemporary techniques, sometimes dramatically different from the old ways, sometimes a blend of both.

— Where, then, do we begin? After what we have been saying in preceding chapters, it will not be surprising to find that most of the current techniques start with body posture and body exercises, all looking toward the longed-for sense that body and spirit are working together, not obstructing each other. Easterners, indeed, believe that it is false to make a clear-cut distinction between body and mind. Moreover, they believe that hidden in the body itself there are "synergic centers," tremendous potentialities for waking the deep, evolutionary mind; and much of yogic discipline is directed to arousing these potential energies.

So it is not surprising that most Eastern disciplines begin with the idea that the very position of the body is important. The fabled lotus posture, for example, has not been chosen simply to torment unaccustomed Western legs and provide material for cartoons. The truth is that once it is learned it gives the body stability and balance and one is left free to turn one's attention inward. It has been found also to be the most relaxed position for the long haul, inducing neither sleep nor wandering mind; it is readily available outdoors or in; it overcomes restlessness; and it seems to have a kind of wisdom of its own.

Reporting on his experiences learning Zen in Japan, the Reverend William Johnston says he felt "deepened" by the half-lotus position, which "somehow impedes discursive reasoning and thinking"; checks the stream of consciousness; detaches us from the very process of thinking; and "is best for going down, down to the center of one's being in imageless and silent contemplation."

The wisdom of this notion turns out to be testable in the science laboratory. In an experiment at Komazawa University in Tokyo, for example, it was discovered that in the stiff-backed, cross-legged lotus position the respiratory rate dropped rapidly and the pulse fell ten to fifteen beats a minute below its normal rate.

Still, it is certainly not an easy position for the average Westerner, especially if he is beyond the age of twenty. I know! All attempts on my own part produce neither relaxation nor meditation. For recalcitrant Westerners like myself, it is recommended that one sit in a chair. One should certainly not vaguely slouch in a lounger, but it is permissible to sit quietly upright in a straight-backed chair, arms resting on the arms of the chair, feet on the floor, relaxed but not relaxed enough to feel sleepy.

Once you are seated, there are a number of routes to take. Some authorities recommend various experiments to make you aware of your body. At Zen Studies we were told to cup our hands just under the abdomen so as to become aware of its rising and falling. Others recommend trying to sense your body outline or trying to be aware of various pressures as you touch your body, cultivating always the sensitivity of your hands.

You will certainly be instructed in breathing exercises. You may be told to take a deep breath, hold it, exhale, and hold it, and then to begin counting your breath—one on the intake, two on the outgo and so on, counting to ten, trying to become one with the feeling of the breath, doing it naturally, not forcing yourself. Such exercises have been found in centuries of practice to aid the journey inward. Breath counting, in fact, is often used as a way to concentrate. Equally certainly, it is relaxing. Generations of speakers and actors have been instructed by speech and drama coaches to practice breathing exercises before going on the stage.

But there is still another significance in breathing exercise. The breath, after all, rises from the roots of being, and it is thought that it "forms a bridge between the conscious and the unconscious systems" and charges the body with a kind of spiritual energy. Then, too, the importance of breathing exercise is no doubt symbolic, since breath is so profoundly related to our very lives and to the rhythm of the body and its interaction with the world around it.

Of course, there are many other possible exercises. Other instructors may tell you to be aware of the beating of the heart or to note the abdomen rising and falling or, if you are on your feet, the foot walking "up, forward, down"; or to tense and then relax the whole body, beginning with the toes and ending up with the different parts of the face; or to be aware of the arm on the chair, feeling its weight, considering its comfort, and, in time, being aware of its lassitude and heaviness. You may also stand on your head and block each nostril alternately while you breathe—if that is in your repertoire!

Sounds also can concentrate our attention, as anyone can discover in music. Complex harmonies wake the mind; simple melodies repeated again and again quiet it. Even natural sounds can help us feel shut off from the distracting world. Who has not experienced this peaceful shut-offness when rain drums rhythmically on the roof, waves break on the shore, fire sighs on the hearth?

This is a purpose—though by no means the only purpose—of chants and mantras, those seemingly meaningless sounds whose usage Westerners find so hard to understand. I know how they feel for I go back in memory to the mixed feelings which were part of my own introduction to lengthy chant.

At the quiet farmhouse in the remote village of Lower Clarence, Nova Scotia, the Arunachala Ashrama, a

New York–based religious organization dedicated to the teachings of the Indian sage Bhagavan Sri Ramana Maharshi, has set up a country subsidiary. It is evening, a summer evening, the sun still hot on the new-mown grass. Outside the window a light early-evening breeze blows in the trees and the grasses of the farmlands where my husband's people, sturdy Baptists all, grew up. But these young people are no Baptists. Rather, those present on this occasion are New York Jews, converted to the faith of the ashram. Numbers of attendants vary, but there are only three on this particular night—the young husband and wife, Matthew and Joan, who maintain the ashram, and their friend Dennis.

I sit with these somewhat esoteric worshipers in what was once the parlor of a sturdy farm family. There is no furniture in the parlor except one straight chair, a hanging plant in the window, a kind of altar arranged on a small table in the corner, with offerings (oranges and flowers) before a picture of the founder. The house is full of his pictures, but it contains also pictures of the prophets and saints of other religions.

We sit on the floor, the young people in lotus position, I in whatever I can manage. They give me a large card containing their ritual chant. The syllables of the chant are musical and flowing: "*Om Shanti, Om Shakti, Hare Rama, Hare Krishna,*" and so forth. They tell me that they are chanting the names of God. The girl is altogether lost in the chant. She chants well in a strong, vibrant voice; Dennis, who looks like a New Testament Apostle, sways with the chant, his lips barely moving. The girl's sweet child-face is free of makeup; her dark hair is pulled back flat on her head; her sari is scrupulously clean. The boys are in blue jeans, but Matthew wears an Indian kind of garment, triangular like a cape. Their eyes are closed; how vulnerable that makes them, for mine are open!

The chant seems unfamiliar and alien to me as it drifts through the open window over the hayfields of this farm village, which is so full of quite different memories for me; and I think how incongruous the sound must seem to a passing farmer driving his cows to pasture or bringing in the hay. Nevertheless, though I cannot identify with it, the chant conveys for me the sense of ancient wisdom in somewhat the same way the Jewish ritual and the traditional Catholic mass do. I have no wish to participate, but I am not restless; only waiting. The chant goes on for half an hour, and now it is drawing to its close. It is ending with a long-drawn, air-vibrating, history-soaked *"Om,"* and suddenly my alienation is ending, and my eyes, surprisingly, fill with tears. No matter that it is a Buddhist syllable. It is still the cry of men everywhere, men on the shepherd's hilltop, at homemade altars, and in great cathedrals: "God, O God, who are you and what are you?"

After that these young people keep silence for thirty minutes, motionless, and this time my eyes too are closed and I think, humbly, "Lord, I bring you my greatest gift, my attention." The silence seems full of voices—the deep supplicant *"Om,"* the *"lama sabachthani"* of Jesus, the Gregorian Chants, the "Now I lay me," the "Our Father Who art in Heaven," the Psalms.

What is the purpose of the chant? In the long *"Om"* I felt, rather than verbally understood, that purpose; but when the service was over I asked Matthew its intent. "We are trying to draw the mind inward," he said, "before we meditate." And thousands of years of experience have shown that such chants—verbally monotonous, making use of syllables symbolically rich and soaked in history —do indeed have that effect.

So does the mantra, which is like the chant, though it may, and often does, consist of a single word. The mantra is perhaps more adaptable to the purposes of the individual seeker, since it may simply be repeated rather than chanted. *Om* itself is often used as a mantra, but the mantra need not have a specific meaning.

No doubt for Americans the most familiar use of the mantra is in Transcendental Meditation. In TM, an individual mantra, usually Sanskrit, is given to each student —and there are now about a hundred thousand students in the United States—and is repeated silently over and over for twenty minutes, twice a day. Teachers of TM are at pains to point out that they are not teaching the student to "concentrate." Rather, as a *Newsweek* reporter put it, they want to let the mantra "float softly through his mind, allowing thought to emerge and dissipate like tiny bubbles of psychological stress."

Almost any simple repetitive sound will have some of the effect of the mantra, but through the ages certain syllables have been found more efficacious than others. Often they are mellifluous and smooth, full of vowels and sonorous *h*'s and *m*'s. One thinks at once of the Tibetan "*Om-Mane-Padme-Hum*." In the end the purpose of the repetitive sound is not only to turn off the external world, to focus one's attention and release the mind from its storms, but to do much more: to relate us at the unconscious level to symbols with mythic power.

The same is true of the objects so often used to help people meditate: the mandala, the cross, the candle flame, and so forth. Most meditative disciplines use objects—at least during the early stages of instruction—to concentrate attention and increase awareness. Again, almost any object can be used—and many are—but centuries of experience have demonstrated that some are better than others.

Preferably, the object has symbolic meaning for the person who is meditating. Obviously, the cross is not as meaningful a symbol for Jews as for Christians; and the menorah, the seven-branched candelabrum of the Jewish tabernacle, has infinitely greater significance for Jews than it could have for Christians.

Human beings are symbol-haunted creatures, and even in the midst of our pragmatic, symbol-destroying age we all use symbols and care about them. A simple homely illustration of that stays in my memory from the Aruna-chala Ashrama. There were many symbols present which did *not* speak to me—flowers and fruit and incense and pictures—but what did speak was a pink seashell left on the mantelpiece by the farm family who originally owned the house. It was a symbol of my childhood and of a child's fantasies of faraway lands, for then almost everyone had such shells, often brought back to Nova Scotia by sea captains from romantic-sounding places—China and Madagascar, Singapore and Hawaii—and we were told, as children, that the sound of the sea was still in the shell. We thought we heard it—surf pounding on tropic shores, the sea singing in the night—and dreamed of the day when all the far reaches of the world would be ours.

But the best objects for meditation have still another quality. They seem to grow in our minds, to "become more rather than less" as we keep on with our intense meditation. Remarking on this, Dr. Naranjo cites such objects as the cross, the Star of David, the rose or the lotus. "Being symbols created by a higher state of consciousness," he says, "they evoke their source and always lead the meditator beyond his ordinary state of mind."

If they lead beyond, they also draw us within them. They seem to spring from the past of the race and lead into the future. One can imagine them as centers around which our actions can flow. In ways we do not understand, their source is deep in the very tissue of human nature. It is even thought that long gazing on symbols of such centrality can change the structure of consciousness. A mandala, for example, is a circular symbol of the universe. Its design may be very intricate and complex, and absorbed attention to a mandala is said to awaken the deeper levels of the mind-brain system. How do we know that it does? We simply find it so.

But whatever the chosen object, its usage is the same. One's eyes are fixed unwaveringly on it, one's attention devoted entirely to it. One thinks of it as having an existence in itself and reaches to it lovingly, not asking what it might be used for. Stay long enough with it and the object itself may seem to change, grow more luminous, more vivid, more "real," reveal something of the nature of objects and of the world they inhabit. It seems to pull us away from the racing surface mind to a creativity that blossoms like an opening rose.

The fourth of the classic disciplines is asceticism. Day and night Siddhartha, the Buddha, sat under the Bo tree; forty days Jesus meditated in the austere and silent desert. From time immemorial, people have sought through hunger, thirst, fatigue and pain for the lightened body, the lucid mind, the disciplined desire. In Zen one may participate in a sesshin—a period of prolonged meditation lasting for days or even weeks—meditating in lotus position for most of each hour ten or twelve hours a day. During this time one eats and sleeps lightly and remains in silence, speaking only to the master teacher. Similarly Christian monks may fast, rise at 3 A.M. for long periods of meditation and prayer, and, like the Trappists, spend most of their lives in silence.

The asceticism of the body may also include the asceticism of the will, the pride, the ego. For example, the young Americans who go to stay for a while in Asiatic monasteries may find themselves rising before dawn to beg their food from door to door, standing silently, not even looking up, as housewives drop bits of food into their alms bowls. They eat these offerings, whatever they may be, during the morning and will often get nothing else during the rest of the day except perhaps a beverage.

What is the point of all this? The answer is so profound that volumes have been written about it. But basically the intent is to let go of the ego, to "lose your life so you may find it." Like the chant and the concentration on the mandala and the yogic exercise, it is an effort to "cleanse the doors of perception," to reduce other claims so that this one claim—the effort to reach the inner room where it is thought that God dwells—can have all our attention.

These are the traditional ways of going to the deep Self, the Self so ancient, yet so new, so rooted in the past, so waited for in the future. We have much to learn from these ways, and they are very much a part of the current movement. But it is doubtful that traditional methods by themselves can answer the needs of contemporary people bedeviled by contemporary problems. This is especially true of Eastern methods. Valuable and rich as they are, they may lead to a kind of abnegation of self and desire which is alien both to Western temperament and to the direction of the Judeo-Christian faiths. Contemporary experimenters believe that people who live in a world as rapidly changing as ours may need new and nontraditional methodologies leading to an exploration of the quality of our own experience and a feeling of freedom to explore it.

In contrast to the quietness of traditional aids to meditation, modern ways of altering consciousness may include very dramatic, spectacular and even noisy techniques. Harvey Cox, for example, points out that the strobe light, so much used today in multimedia events, works because it "interrupts the smooth flow of visual images and chops them into shredded instants." So, he says, we're constantly making new takes. Since our eyes and brains can't go that fast, we are driven to letting the "images flow in unsorted, thus giving the mind a startling new stimulus."

The range of contemporary experimentation is, in fact, enormous. It includes devices not available to us in the past for inducing altered states of consciousness—for example, the electroencephalograph for biofeedback and brain-wave exercises; blown-up slides and photographic montage; instruments for delivering exotic sounds.

Such modern tools help at the Foundation for Mind Research, whose founders, in fact, began their work by an exhaustive study of the effect of psychedelic drugs. They also, as noted earlier, use fairly elaborate audiovisual environments: kaleidoscopic slides on screens which are semicircular so that they seem to wrap around the subject; sensory deprivation; stroboscopic light; and a modern version of the ancient witch's cradle, a version they describe as essentially a metal swing or pendulum in which the research subject stands upright, supported by broad bands of canvas, wearing blindfold "goggles." In this position he is carried forward and backward, side to side, and so forth. The subject tends to lose his spatial referents as well as his temporal ones, may feel as though he were "flying through whorls, vortices and mists," and finally enters a world "of his own internal imagery."

Dr. Masters is also working on the use of prolonged rhythmic movements. "I find," he told me, "that after several hours you break down the body image. There is no longer a sense of the body as such. It may begin to feel as if it is made of particles of energy, or it may begin to feel as if it is made of tongues of fire. . . . There is no more fatigue of any kind; it can go on for hours after hours. The body feels completely light. All the heaviness goes out of it. . . . When one reaches this state—a feeling that the body is made of particles of energy, that the grosser human body is gone and a more subtle human body has come to be—then the experience assumes the transcendental dimension and you come very close to feeling that this body is much more the reality than the other body, and that if you could get to this state of consciousness and retain it, perhaps you could heal that other body, and perhaps you would be resistant to trauma."

But there is another kind of "newness" available, not through instrumentation but through the researches of depth psychology and the very contemporary understanding of the unconscious; and it often takes the form of training in *mental imagery* through meditation.

Mind Games, Masters and Houston's recent work on directed meditation—even deep trance—leading to altered states of consciousness or deliberately evoking imagery describes innumerable such voyages. For example, you may be told—the voice gentle, hypnotic, leading you—that you are going back to a dream you had when you were a small child, a dream that was more like going into another world than it was like your usual dream. Dreaming, you get out of your bed and find a door in the back of the closet. In the dream, the door opens and you pass through it and stand at the top of ancient stone steps, and in the dim light you go down the staircase, not afraid, to dark water, black as ink, where a small boat is waiting; and you float away in the blackness, rocking gently on the water, till you "pass out of a cavernous opening and into a warm sunlight." And then you drift down and down, and along the bank the birds are singing and there is freshly cut grass in the fields; and so you journey on.

Or you may be asked, in a far more complex meditation, to experience earth, air, water, or the moment of dying, the "great sacred mystery of dying," a moment to be free of weaknesses and move into strength. "You will open your eyes then," you are told, "and behold the world as it is in that moment when you are born again."

As described earlier, a somewhat different, perhaps more self-directed program goes on at Dialogue House in New York, where Dr. Ira Progoff leads people in weekend seminars and summer workshops, using the keeping of a psychological journal—he calls it the "Intensive Journal"—as part of the process.

The journal is used as a mirror for reflecting back the inner nature of our lives; as "an instrument and technique by which persons can discover within themselves the resources they did not know they possessed." You may be asked to go into deep meditation by breathing: breathe in and out three times, then hold. Perhaps you will also be asked to use a mantra. You may be asked to identify a period in your life which seemed to you a unit and write about this period of time; or to identify ten or twelve steppingstones in your life; or to meditate on intersections in your life where things could have gone one way or the other; or to dialogue with people, living or dead, who have—or had—an inner importance in your own life; or to dialogue with your own body; or with your profession; or with a project you have been working on and in which you have come to an impasse; or to go down into the well of yourself in order to discover there the continuity and meaning of your life.

In what he calls "twilight imagery," you may be helped to go into deep meditation and to project the imagery which then rises on a mental screen, searching for the meaning of what comes. Often such inwardness produces profound symbolic images. Sometimes, indeed, an individual is helped to continue in this way the imagery of a dream he has had and almost understood.

For example, one woman, a Mrs. White, who was searching for the solution of various problems in personal relationships dreamed in a heavy atmosphere like Greek tragedy that a man was approaching his home and, as he did so, a woman stepped out of the house and said dramatically, "All is different. I am blind now." Returning in twilight imaging to the atmosphere of her dream, she had the feeling, Dr. Progoff reports, that if they could only dive into a nearby swimming pool her blindness would vanish and she would see again. But the man was reluctant and even adamant, and finally she dived in alone and swam by herself, down, down into the bottom of the pool. Now—underwater—she does see, and she feels very relaxed and comforted. When she swims to the surface again she can even see much more clearly than ever before. "Everything is very light and brilliant," she says. "The air is just full of sunlight. It is dancing with sunlight, and distant mountains are sharp and close."

People too; now she can see people in a special way. She can look at people and see way behind their eyes. "She sees beneath the rocky ledge under the earth. She sees a stream of water moving under it, and now she sees wells coming up from it."

As is his custom, Dr. Progoff asked her to record as much of the imagery as she could. Seeking to do so, she again found herself deep in the pool. She realized that "diving into the pool was the equivalent of going down into the depths of her psyche. It was saying to her that when she lived on the surface of things she was as one blind, but when she went into the dimension of depth her eyes opened and she could see."

Clearly the goal of such imagery, whether at Dialogue House or elsewhere, is expanded awareness of what is taking place in the depths of the psyche, and awareness as well of realities that are beyond the range of our everyday vision.

Finally, contemporary methods use a great many group activities. Group activity is very old, but in the past it was usually confined largely to disciples—people who were learning their way into lifelong disciplines. Today many people not so disciplined—people even who are coming together only briefly—meditate in groups and, without speech, often feel a tide of love flowing among them. Group meditation is common in many different contexts: amongst people working together at a common social-welfare task, who pause and find their way together to a deep place where they are one; in groups meeting perhaps weekly for the express purpose of meditating; in communes, where it is often a daily practice.

Such meditation is, in fact, part of the strength of the most enduring communes. A movie of such a commune provoked considerable discussion at the last annual meeting of the American Academy of Psychoanalysis. The commune was in Oregon, in a forest of huge primeval trees. The young people who formed the commune grew their own food, built their own houses. At meditation time, a bearded young man struck a gong. One girl, hands in her lap, led in the Lord's Prayer. They repeated it together with bent heads, reverently. Then they sat quietly, silently meditating.

One bitter wintry night not long ago, I followed a

crowd into a meditation service at St. Luke's Chapel in lower Manhattan. The service was not church-sponsored. The multitude of people who crowded in were simply using the church facilities. They started arriving long before the appointed evening hour—mostly young people, but a substantial sprinkling, too, of older ones. They streamed into the basement meeting room, taking off their shoes before they entered. They are called the Hilda Meditation Group, because they are led by a woman named Hilda. "She has been to India," my neighbor whispers softly. "She has a great devotional life."

But she is not yet here, and I use the time to look around me. The room is filling rapidly. In time there will be only standing room, and that in the hall. There are pictures on the wall: Jesus, Buddha, Krishna. "He's a god," my neighbor whispers again.

People chant and sway as they wait. Many of them—perhaps most—are sitting on the floor. A few clap hands in rhythm. Hilda comes in quietly: a woman in a purple sari, masses of dark hair, shapeless, white-faced, not young; but I am moved by her eyes, which are deep and ageless, weary, but visionary. The chant increases. Many do not seem to know the words, but a devout group—who are sitting on the floor—do, and they perform it with eyes closed.

Afterward they sing melodiously,

> Take me to the Lord,
> Wonderful he seems.
> There is no greater savior
> Than my Lord to me.

The melody is very haunting; people clap in rhythm, and a young girl sings and plays a guitar. I remember suddenly how it is when one is young and full of longing, and it comes to me that I have not in decades felt this sweet sorrow of the young. Perhaps many people come for the girl's sweet singing.

Someone has brought Hilda white flowers, and she is appreciative. She speaks now, but very softly, and she cannot be heard at the back of the room. Someone brings her a baby who has been fussing. She holds him lovingly and puts her hand on his head. He is quiet and peaceful.

I estimate that there are more than three hundred here. They come and go informally, though softly. Hilda speaks again, asking a collection for starving people, and a paper shopping bag goes the rounds. A beautiful, elegant woman in a mink stole goes by and seats herself on the floor. Hilda's remarks—which I can hear now because I have gone up to stand in a doorway to listen—are informal and somewhat amusing, and she remains seated. Often she smilingly addresses someone in the audience, and the person responds. They are like disciples who gather around. The girl with the baby goes out, duly saluted by the audience. Hilda is telling stories at which the audience laughs delightedly. A curly-haired young man wearing a Jewish skullcap sits in front of me, and a regular attendant near me whispers that almost everyone in the audience is a Christian or a Jew.

They sing, "Rama, Rama, Rama, Jesus, Jesus, Jesus"; and I smile, thinking of how horrified my minister father would be at such a juxtaposition. A visitor from the Midwest reads eloquently the poetry of the Indian poet Kabir. "'Everything is swinging,'" he reads, "'water, angels, animals, insects—also heaven, earth and human beings.'" The audience loves it, and many shout, "Wow!" But when Hilda says, "Shall we have more or shall we have meditation?" a chorus of voices cries, "Meditation"; and they sink into silence while Hilda walks up and down the aisles, telling them how to breathe, how to go down into themselves.

There are traditional ways and contemporary ways; and finally there is *your* way, which is the most important of all. Instruction, it is true, is valuable, and people who want to meditate seriously should have it if possible. But once instruction is over most of us will have to continue on our own. And if meditation is to be a true style in our lives, all of us, instructed or not, will need to understand its basic skills.

Moreover, techniques obviously differ for different people. Some of us are turned off by one thing, turned on by another. The Reverend William Johnston, describing his efforts to teach seminary students in this country to sit in the silence of zazen, admitted that many complained that "just sitting" was somehow driving them into isolation; and he decided therefore to begin and end the sessions with singing—a method which turned out to be a useful concession to Western restlessness.

And then, though training is useful, people *have* been meditating on their own since the beginning of time. It must be remembered that Quakers, uninstructed except by "the Inner Light," have left behind voluminous journals detailing singular and beautiful experience in meditation; and that the best test of good meditating, its effect on daily life, is passed triumphantly by a host of people doing it on their own.

Moreover, it is probably true to say that no two people meditate in the same way any more than they work, play or love in the same way. So in the end whatever technique works for you is fine for *you*. But a few things are basic.

For one thing, we need to come to meditation open-minded, free of predictions and demands. We should not be meditating with the determination to use it to get rid of bad habits, or to solve our problems, or to achieve peace of mind, or to have exotic extrasensory "highs," or even to come upon the marvelous change which is satori. All these things may happen, but to start with that expectation is to forgo the openness of the journey and to forget that its most important goal is *enlightenment*—an enlightenment whose form no one can prescribe or foresee.

It *is* desirable, too, to *set aside a time and choose a place*. To be sure, people can meditate in a moment snatched over lunch, in the time you can induce your seat mate on a commuter train not to talk to you. But it is difficult—particularly difficult for twentieth-century Americans, since we must surely be the most time-conscious people that ever lived. For us time is a goad, a sting, an enemy. We always know how fast it is going and how much we have to do. We rush on the job; we rush to it. We rush home again. The strokes of the pendulum seem to measure off our lives, and we hear the minutes ticking, telling us how fast time is fleeing from us, telling us how much we have left to do.

So if we are to counter the constant pressure of schedules and schemes, of noise and clocks, of inner conflict and old habit, we need to set aside a quiet time each day, usually at least a half hour. This has to be done consistently, too, because the results are as cumulative as those of other skills. Moreover, when we set aside a regular time the habit is formed, the mind is ready. Experts often recommend an hour early in the morning for its solitude and for the quiet and serenity which comes before the bustle of the day, and for its symbolic value as well. The early-morning hours are like a rebirth: we are ahead of the people-rush, the mind is open and ready, we experience a world new-born.

Place is important for the same reason that time is, and for other reasons as well. I have seen people meditate with considerable concentration in the subway or even behind a potted palm at a cocktail party. But even the young, who have long ago demonstrated their ability to study tomorrow's lessons to the tune of a rock band, move to the desert or the forest for serious meditation; and gurus, who can transport themselves more easily into the silence of meditation than we can, still choose remoteness and silence, the hermitage, the forest, the lonely shore, the quiet room.

Place matters because *solitude* matters. We are trying to leave behind the familiar worries and tasks which often seem to haunt home base; to separate the meditator from the usual round of daily activities, to find our way to a solitude where time is not, where it has no existence. But place matters also for another reason. It matters because certain places more than others carry an aura of tranquillity, peace and beauty or by their mystery and strangeness turn off our daily preoccupations. The desert, for example, has a long tradition as a sensitizing place for meditation. Jesus, we are told, spent forty days in the wilderness, and it is written that there in the long and hard silence he faced the human temptation to use his great gifts for himself, and he put behind him the kingdoms of the world and the glory of them.

The desert is still a preferred place for silence. The Spiritual Life Institute in Arizona was not set up in the high desert accidentally. It is there, says a descriptive pamphlet, because life in the desert, for all its disadvantages, offers the clearest and most merciless light in the world for seeing things as they really are, which the founders of the Institute define as the act of contemplation.

It is true. The "merciless" penetrating light—so bright the stones seemed to shine from inside—speaks of eternal things. So does the silence, the great expanse of sky, and —in Arizona—the noble, rose-red mountains, each rising abruptly and alone from the desert. And then there are the forces which speak so endlessly of death and life: the silence; the great expanse of sky and land; the great leaves of the cactus with thorns that can kill; the brown earth where deadly snakes roam; the ridged, twisted, corrugated trunks of the cedar trees; the innumerable hard and thorny bushes; the gray-green leaves; the tall dry spikes of the yuccas; and the myriad tiny bright plants which spring triumphantly from every little crack in the barren earth.

I knew a sixteen year old whose place of solitude was the streets of a sleeping city in the night. If rain waked him in the night, he would rise and walk in it, a copy of his beloved Conrad or Poe in his pocket to remind him by its touch of other worlds and ways. When I was fourteen or fifteen, I too felt a special need for solitude, for an untouched place where I could simply "be." We lived then, my parsonage parents, my brother and I, in a village by the wild and stormy Bay of Fundy in Nova Scotia. Sometimes the shore itself was a place to go to, especially on a foggy day when no one was about and the surf rolled in slowly and calmly without its habitual violence. But I found another very special aloneness. There was a deserted house not far from us, and behind it, encircled by the encroaching forest, an apple orchard which had gone wild. On spring mornings with the blossoms on the trees,

I often slipped out of the house at dawn and watched the sun rise over the forest from the top branches of a blossoming tree. In silence, not consciously thinking, how easy it was to feel the bond between this rising, flowering world and my own just-beyond-a-child self.

In adult life, I remember the Nystien Hotel in Norway: a quiet, bare, infinitely peaceful room; goats and sheep going up the snowy mountains; the barren, treeless terrain; the almost constant daylight; the lonely ski huts. I remember a Quaker meetinghouse in Connecticut, a beautiful, simple sanctuary with no religious symbols, no decorations, only the flames of the fireplace reflected in the polished floor.

· What these places all seem to hold in common is that they answer to the need to be alone or to feel alone, the need for more space or the feeling of space, the need for a chance to be merged in whatever one is experiencing. But place has another significance. If one can have a special place for meditation, then the moment one enters it the mind accepts it as the place to leave the world behind; memory teaches that this is the realm of silence. It is for that reason that Zen Buddhists urge that there should be a sanctuary near you, always ready, cushions there to sit on, incense ready to light, pictures of sages or saints—or other symbols—on hand to create a meditative mood.

˙ Place and time chosen, you may want to borrow a mantra or adopt one of your own to shut out the world and find your way to the deep Self. Almost any simple repetitive sound will have a relaxing effect. I find efficacious the long phrase "Relax, relax, go down, go down into the deep well of myself." An elderly Quaker told me that he himself concentrated on a symbol of goodness, a symbol he chose for himself. Some Quakers make a regular practice of inwardly reciting the Lord's Prayer, the Beatitudes, a psalm, and so forth, to put themselves in a proper frame of mind for meditation.

. Posture too *is* important. For one thing, if we are physically tense and our nerves are jangling, our bodies will interrupt meditation with a clamor about pain in this muscle or that, or about headaches, stiff necks and so forth. So if the lotus position is not for you, sit as suggested earlier, in a straight-backed chair, feet flat on the floor, arms on the arms of the chair, and count your breathing: in-out, in-out, in-out, hold, and so on.

· In your early experiences of meditation you will be easily discouraged. The emptying of the mind will not go well. Other thoughts will inevitably rise during the silent contemplation, the saying of the mantra, the exercises in breathing. No matter. Permit them, but do not indulge them. Simply watch them go by, and come back as soon as you can to the mandala or the mantra or whatever you were concentrating on.

· You will find some attention to *diet* useful, too. Just as the athlete eats special foods suited to muscular strength and development, so the meditator, seeking instead a lightened body and a lucid mind, will be helped by a spare diet, rich in fruits and vegetables, and at the least will find a brief period of trying it a learning experience in self-understanding. For the most important thing to be said about the ascetic way of life is that it teaches simplicity, instructs in priorities. One of the great discoveries of a period spent in meditation in a retreat is the discovery of how little we really need. "Things" are delightful, and there is no reason for all of us to be ascetics, or for any of us to be so all the time; but we must be in control of things, not the other way around.

Arizona offered a perfect illustration of this as of so much else. Good things were not despised at the Spiritual Life Institute, merely kept in their place. For example, there was rarely wine, because there was no money to buy it, but when somebody made them a present of it everyone was delighted. And if breakfast and lunch were sketchy, to say the least, dinner was usually a delight—often even gourmet, in spite of the fact that it usually had to be made from what someone had donated. At other times food was of little importance, and one absently ate crackers and peanut butter or sometimes nothing. How disturbed I was when I arrived, fresh from the thing-oriented society outside! But one morning was all it took to dispel this clinging to goods and chattels. Alone on my patio, invisible, silent, unsolicited by anyone, I could endlessly watch a lizard traveling up the stones, or ponder a book slow sentence by slow sentence. No breakfast or lunch to go to, because none was served. In the cupboard of my house there was food, unremarkable, easy to get, undemanding, but no meals interrupted your thought unless you wished them to.

There are other ways too of approaching meditation—ways available to all of us. One can practice the art of "being present"—committing oneself totally to a given moment in time: to the person one is with, to the worship one is part of, to the sky or sea one is looking at, to the music one is hearing. In any case the point is to find your *own* way to the here and now, your own way to shutting out the world so that you can reach the inner self which is your own kingdom and nobody else's. Experiment, too, on yourself to find out what *stops* you from concentrating, and what helps you. Don't forget that symbols and objects are only a technique and that what we are trying for is attention *itself*, awareness *itself*.

Perhaps you may want to meditate with others. Group silence can be more effective than solitary silence. Indeed, it sets the stage for the most profound communion possible to human beings. It is as though we multiplied our experience by sharing it; as though the massed feelings, thoughts and searchings of others could somehow become part of and strengthen our own; as though we were, in some way, expanding each other's space. Moreover, many contemporary groups provide another sort of help, a sharing of feeling, responses, problems in meditation. Hearing other people report on their feelings, you find you are more in touch with your own, better able to articulate them if only to yourself. It helps; and it is available almost everywhere. Even if an experienced leader cannot be found, a group of people anywhere can come together in Quaker-style meetings—sitting quietly in an atmosphere conducive to meditation, and speaking when something rises from your inmost self that you want to say.

At its simplest, meditation is for everyone who feels that he or she is "not getting anywhere," not finding answers to the questions that trouble him, not discovering a meaning in life. It is for the people who feel a distance between themselves and others, a tiredness without physical cause, a lack of purpose, a lack of wholeness. It can be a systematic illumination of hidden places, of what else besides the obvious is going on in our lives, of the manner of our interaction with the world and other people, of what Pasternak called "the territory of conscience." The individual meditating may acquire maturity and self-understanding, a capacity to sense how other human beings compose their world, and a vivid awareness of his own being.

At its most profound, it opens the gates of life and eternity, lets us become at last what we truly are. It may even change the face we show the world, says the anonymous author of the beautiful classic of mysticism, *The Cloud of Unknowing.* Meditation transforms the body and makes it beautiful, he tells us. Even the most ugly person, he says, will become fair and attractive to everyone; his face will be suffused with joy, and a certain grace and peace will accompany his every action.

Finally, disciplined though it is, meditation has a close alliance with freedom; for the space the meditator moves in is wider than that of the nonmeditator, the reach is farther, the trust in his own insight greater. Have we not, all of our lives, put up walls to keep out the great rush of our own authenticity? Now at last we can take them down and give ourselves permission to become what we are.

But though the rewards of meditation are great and cumulative, this skill, like all skills, has a price. Even its smallest gains have a cost, and for its mountaintop experiences that cost may be a big one. It requires discipline and *discrimination;* no greater disservice can be done to this new movement than an indiscriminate acceptance of everything.

And, finally, as we shall see in the next chapter, it needs to make its peace with the *world of action.* Powerful and gifted as it is, the movement will die if it feeds on itself, becomes ingrown, fails to return to the world the evolutionary wisdom and insight it has won.

CHAPTER 7

The Joyful Rhythm

~~~~~~

Once when I was a little girl, much addicted to daydreaming in solitary treetops and on lonely beaches, I encountered an old fisherman working on his boat on what I thought of as "my" beach.

"Saw you here yesterday," he said.

"Uh huh," I acknowledged, emerging briefly from whatever inward recesses I had been enjoying.

"Good place," he said. "Sea's always a good place. Don't make me lonely either. But it don't do to stay too long. Gets in your blood and you can't leave it."

He was right. In the same way, people can be so enamored of the sweet magic of the inward world that they do not want to leave it. It *can* be a copout, a deliberate flight from the real, from the task of making the world a better place to live in. In the face of apparent imminent disaster on our planet, how easy it would be to retreat into one's own private fantasy; how easy to ignore the pain and conflict in the world, to refuse to take part in the struggle for dignity and freedom and concentrate

simply on the health of one's own soul! The land of
Circe is a temptation to all of us in time of trouble,
and it is likely that some of today's meditators, some of
our communes, some of our self-made gurus, are indeed
taking such refuge.

Americans will not welcome the apostles of the inward
journey if this explosive, exciting new movement is made
to appear as a way of retreating from the world, foregoing
needed action, leaving it all for the other fellow to do. I
feel a certain sympathy with the business executives who
reacted indignantly to a proposal to substitute relaxing
meditation for the customary coffee break. Writing in
letters to the *Harvard Business Review,* which had, in its
July-August issue of 1974, published an article advocating
this way of taking the stress out of business, they said
that stress would be "sorely missed," that it was needed
to get things done. One letter writer said he often went
to great extremes to instill stress reactions in his sub-
ordinate executives.

There is much to be said for that point of view. If
peace of mind is all that meditation can give us, it will
lose its appeal when times are better; and instead of being
an evolutionary step in the development of man's consciousness, it will more easily contribute to turning back
the clock.

There are meditation buffs as there are encounter buffs
—people who spend their lives going from one mystic
or psychic experience to the other—and such dilettantism
is a temptation to that legion of people who want only
to be comforted, to find some anodyne for their pain.
Moreover, serious meditators, whose maturity prevents
such a childlike search, have their own temptation, a
temptation which appeals especially to the noble and

sensitive. For them the exalted experience of purification and of the knowing of God carries such a stamp of authenticity, not to say radiance, that to achieve it can seem enough for a lifetime's task. "Lord, it is good for us to be here," said the disciples to Jesus on the Mount of Transfiguration; and they pleaded—in vain—to stay and "build three tabernacles."

Certainly there is room for a group of people—monks, mystics, scholars—whose concerns are more or less divorced from action, who exist on the fringe of secular life, making discoveries which, like those of the pure scientist, have no present practical use, but whose findings look to a long future and, in the meantime, deepen fundamental human experience and are like a transfusion of the atmosphere.

But the risk for all of us who want to stay on the Mount of Transfiguration is that we will develop a smug separateness; the hubris of a status at one with God; loss of touch with a world of other humans. It is a real risk; for meditators who do not use what they have won not only deprive society but hinder their own psychic growth, suffering often from the cranky pride of elitism. If I am concentrated entirely on my own inward self and I do not take the trouble to know you, there is always the chance that I will see myself as a superior being, riding on the wings of God, while you grub about sweeping floors and selling stocks. Such a notion is a much greater loss to me and to my growth than it is to you.

Most human beings cannot and should not spend their lives as hermits on a mountaintop. There is a passion and earthiness, a love and service which is also life. There are problems to be solved, problems of life and death, conflict and grief, problems near to every human heart. There is work to be done. There is a world out there—a huge, sinful, loving, joyous, working, suffering world—and the people who are sensitive enough, noble enough, to find their way to God are the very ones who are most needed there.

Moreover, it is not an accident that the inward life is often especially cultivated in poverty-stricken countries; in times of crisis when people feel particularly helpless and powerless; in tradition-bound institutions which prescribe saving one's own soul at the expense of one's fellow men. When human beings languish too much over their own salvation, justice does not get done and the plea for human rights is met with callousness, indifference, or at best inept action.

Recently I reread Dorothy Wordsworth's beautiful journals—full of reverie and communication with nature, tranquil pages in which the day is eventful if one has seen unusual cloud banks in the sky, or moonlight on the water. It is all beautiful; but servants, and not the visionaries, are doing the hard work, and while the poor begging at the door are given a penny, their hard lives are never questioned.

When I was a little girl my mother was what was then known as an elocutionist; that is, she recited—and well too—stories and monologues, which delighted her audiences. One of her favorite pieces told the story of a ragged, hungry boy on whom a beautiful lady bestowed a radiant smile and a bunch of flowers. Overwhelmed with happiness, he quit begging for the day and rushed back to the hut where he lived with and somehow supported a little brother who was dying of a painful disease. Once there, he aroused the nearly moribund child with cries of "Prop your eyes wide open, Joey" (the line is exact in my memory) and then—oh, wonder of wonders! —laid his flowers on the ragged blanket. The child promptly died, but not until he had experienced a moment of bliss which presumably made it all worthwhile and no doubt assured the kind lady her reward in heaven.

It was characteristic of the decade that this gruesome text disturbed neither my mother—though she was far ahead of her time in her loving concern for people in trouble—nor her audiences, who usually wept copiously. It is a good thing to remember when we tell ourselves that our world is getting worse and worse, for it is unlikely that there is an audience today which would hear such a story politely. Nevertheless, today's meditators are not entirely free of such escapism. In fact, there may be a contemporary parallel in some present-day communes. Many, it is true, are activist, but others are frankly foxholes and bomb shelters from the world their denizens would like to dismiss.

Such attitudes if widespread would promptly destroy the inward revolution itself. "I mistrust the mystic experience," a friend of mine wrote me after she had spent a day on one of the great marches in Washington back in the sixties, "because it is essentially an incommunicable experience which can be barren of anything but spiritual satisfaction for the one involved."

Insofar as she is right, the inward journey, the heavenly vision, can be the enemy of life rather than its ally. There is a parable whose author I've been trying to find for years. It is a story of a trainload of people who journeyed endlessly onward, living, eating, playing, loving and enjoying each other. This life seemed fine to them except that from time to time one of their number would inexplicably vanish from the train and never return. At last the nar-

rator himself is whisked away, and he finds himself outside in air and sunlight, beauty and wonder. There is a
Presence to greet him, and he turns to this Presence with
the awestruck whisper "Why didn't you tell us? Why
haven't we known so that we could wait with joy for this
day?" To which the Presence replies, "Would you have
found life with your friends good if I had? Would you
have loved each other and helped each other, played
together and worked together?"

Whatever is to come in the future, we are now in this
life and it is this life we must live, and live with gusto
and joy. So it is fair and right that the meditator will in
time be asked to justify his withdrawal by throwing light
on the timeless questions of good and evil and by participating in the daily anguish and conflict of his fellow
humans. Indeed, for the average person whose life is
lived out, not in the monastery but in secular society, the
action which results from meditation is as important as
the meditation itself. Someone has to right the world's
wrongs, and not many of them are visible for righting
in the desert. Dag Hammarskjöld, the United Nations' second Secretary General, who in his own life so thoroughly
combined the inward journey and the outward one, wrote
that "in our era the road to holiness necessarily passes
through the world of action."

So it is fortunate that the dichotomy between meditation and action which is constantly stressed by the critics
of the meditative life is wholly false. It always has been.
It is even a mistake to suppose that this is the way the
saints and mystics lived in the past. True, there are a few
who have done so—and should—just as there are a few
pure scientists; but for every one, saint or mystic, who
has spent his life on his own visions, there are a dozen

who have brought back the fruits of their contemplation to a longing world.

The great Western mystics have, for the most part, been energetic and influential. Even monasticism has historically been far more activist than is generally understood. Harvey Cox describes the historic world of the monastery as a life quite different from what most of us imagine it to be. "Monasticism," he says, "was actually an immense and multifarious series of experiments in alternative community life styles. The monks prayed and meditated . . . sang, read, composed music, copied and illuminated manuscripts, studied every classical language and discipline, developed new agricultural techniques, provided solace and hospitality, worked, ate, and drank together in thousands of different communal patterns. They served, taught, nursed, prayed for, and contributed to the life of the commonweal. The different monastic orders embodied numberless fantasies of how human beings could live together in love and mutuality."

It is equally true outside the monastery. Gandhi was a saintly ascetic who spent much time in solitude and inwardness, yet he invented and carried to victory a powerful political-action weapon. Dag Hammarskjöld, who operated with such great administrative skill to help small and neutral nations and to seek peace, left behind a book, *Markings*, his private journal, which scarcely mentioned Khrushchev or the Suez or the other huge international dramas of his life, and was instead preoccupied with what he called his "negotiations with God." One cannot read this journal without realizing that it was this lifelong inwardness which was the source of his courage, compassion and wisdom.

The Judeo-Christian faiths especially stress emerging

from altar and Torah to plunge into the maelstrom of human needs, to struggle for a better world. One thinks of the two Commandments obligatory for both faiths: "Thou shalt love the Lord thy God with all thy heart and with all thy mind and with all thy soul; and thy neighbor as thyself." Writing in the *Christian Century*, Dr. Gabriel Fackre, professor of theology at Andover-Newton Theological School, says: "The spirituality issuing out of the Judeo-Christian matrix struggles toward contemplation accompanied rather than polarized with action and speech. It seeks the Presence in the midst of social and political ferment." The life of Pope John XXIII is a perfect illustration. He will be remembered as the Pope of action, if only because of his great gatherings of bishops that did so much to transform and update the church. But his autobiographical writing is one long testimony to the vigorous, constant, inward exercise which sustained the outward life of perhaps the most activist of this century's popes.

Quakers have absolutely personified this combination of spirit within and love for each other. Their faith is based on the conviction of George Fox, their founder, that there is a light in every man, "that of God in every man"; that one must spend part of one's life in meditation and silence to find that light, and that then it must be expressed in daily living.

John Youngblut, who has had a long and distinguished record with the American Friends Service Committee, including a period as director of the International Student House in Washington, D.C., now on the teaching staff at Pendle Hill, a religious and social-problems school in Pennsylvania, says that historically it was on "the strength of the recurring mystic consciousness of Jesus' presence in the gathered company" that Quakers could fling down the gauntlet to the establishment in both church and state, "and court excommunication, imprisonment, even loss of life." America's own special Quaker, William Penn, wrote, "wherefore stand still in thy mind; wait to feel something that is divine to prepare and dispose thee to worship God truly and acceptably"; yet he also superintended the laying out of the city of Philadelphia and spent a life in public service.

Quakers, in fact, have constantly alternated their Sabbath stillness with a judicious and effective struggle for peace and for the elimination of the causes of war, and they have fought consistently against slavery, racism and poverty. The American Friends Service Committee is a world-renowned organization, which was set up to provide direct relief for victims of World War I. Since then the Committee has fed refugees and cared for the wounded in all armed conflicts. For a time after World War I, the Friends fed more than one million German children every day. Quakers have also been active through the Service Committee in studying the causes of international tension, arranging conferences between diplomats, resettling refugees, sponsoring foreign-exchange students, and so forth. In Youngblut's view, this energy and power has sprung directly from "the peculiar Quaker blend of the mystical, the prophetic and the evangelical during those periods when we have been most ourselves."

If this has been especially characteristic of Quakers and of the Judeo-Christian faiths in general, it remains unfair to say that the so-called Eastern faiths are bound up in a lifetime of Nirvana-seeking and navel-watching and nothing else. Exploring a number of them for this book, I was surprised to find how many of them do stress the rhythm of inwardness and action.

Zen, for example, is often practical, emphasizing the

value of work. "In Zen's emphasis on self-reliance and pragmatic concerns, its clear awareness of the dangers of intellectualism, its appeal to personal experience rather than philosophical speculation," wrote Philip Kapleau, "Americans can surely find much that is useful and naturally congenial"; and Hal Bridges reminds us that in the Buddhist faith "one who has attained enlightenment, but has postponed the supreme enlightenment of fully perfected Buddhahood in order to keep a vow to help all beings attain spiritual freedom, is called a Bodhisattva. . . . His heart overflows with compassion and love for all that lives. He is his brother's keeper; he knows that in Oneness he *is* his brother."

The purpose of Ananda Marga too, I was told, was to maintain not only a journey within but a journey without —into the social and economic realm. "In order to develop spiritually," the young leaders of the movement told me, "we have to help our fellow men and relieve their suffering."

History knows nothing better than this interplay of inwardness and loving action, and it is no mystery that it works so well. We have only to look about us in the natural world to realize that life is meant to be lived in the rhythm of action and inwardness, engagement and retreat. The seed lies fallow, then grows into the plant that helps to feed the world. The stream on its way to the sea idles in tranquil pools and then rushes on to bear the laden traffic of the world's oceans. The sun sets and the quiet night appears; the sun rises and the day rushes in.

As life is naturally rhythmic in nature, so it is for us. We too need the earth of our deepest selves, the place where seeds are nurtured and roots grow, the primeval place where the sense of origin and the thrust of the life force teaches us our linkage with the living world and the power behind it; but we also need to burst into the sunlight, show ourselves to the world and bring nourishment and flavor, joy and knowledge to our fellow human beings. The rhythm of people and solitude, solitude and people; inwardness and outwardness, the transcendent and the activist—this is the joyful rhythm, the as-it-was-meant-to-be mode of life which satisfies our longings and uses all that we have to give.

At Esalen, where we had all practiced many forms of meditation, a middle-aged furniture salesman sat next to me at the lunch table. Why had he come, I asked, and had he ever been to such gatherings before?

"Oh, yes," he said quickly. "Often." And then he pondered the first question for a moment. He had come, he said, "to live more fully, to have more to give."

"You do not think of it as escape?" I prodded.

He was shocked. "Oh, no," he said, "We are not retreating from life when we meditate. We are advancing *into* life."

On the eve of his departure for the silence of the Trappist monastery, the priest-psychologist Henri Nouwen, an activist teacher at Yale Divinity School, went further. "I see spiritual life," he said, "not as a retreat from the world, but as being set free to be in the world with power."

Indeed, one of the marvels of the inward life is that there we *do* learn to deal with power. Brave men emerge ready to battle against injustice and cruelty and indifference without having to ask themselves what the consequences will be; ready, too, to leave security behind if security is an obstacle in their path. To be deprived of inwardness is even, in fact, to be deprived of a true outward life, for only the understanding found in the depths of the self can lead us directly through our own experience to the larger world of the experience of others. "In deep solitude I find the gentleness with which I can love my brother," wrote Thomas Merton.

No, time is not wasted in meditation. Nonetheless, the life lived *only* in the inner place where the Self is nurtured is half lived. "We're all in the world together," argues John Peer Nugent, writing in the Spiritual Life Institute's magazine, *Desert Call.* "To duck out for self-restricted areas is not what He had in mind—He who left His contemplative quarters to walk among us in the mainstream of New Testament history! . . . Aren't we talking about a form of cultural apartheid where the few refuse to recognize the worth of many?" If we are, then the brilliantly promising inward revolution will die in its infancy.

But I don't think we are. No one wants to scrap an economist and put a Buddhist monk in his place. We need them both. Moreover, experiences and relationships in the outward life illuminate the inward one as surely as our inward selves light our outer path. Indeed, our very birth separates us from solitude and insures that we can never truly be severed from the "web of human connections which increasingly engage us until death." "We meet God in human affairs as well as in our hidden hearts and, if we only cultivate our soul's garden, our lives will not bear fruit," wrote Parker Palmer, a Quaker who is dean of studies at Pendle Hill.

Moreover, the "outward life" too is full of beauty. Just as the inward life should not be thought of as peace and nothing else, so the outward life cannot be defined simply as "action." Rather, it encompasses everything with which you emerge into the world from the journey you have made to the wellsprings of life. It encompasses the joy with which you walk about making the world shine for others as well as for yourself; and it encompasses the lucid thinking, the conscious, informed judgment which takes you to the core of problems.

Indeed, one of the arguments against the use of psychedelic drugs as a means of obtaining the exalted highs of inward discovery is that their usage does not normally lead to action. "They give access," said Aldous Huxley—himself a cautious but interested experimenter with such drugs—"to a contemplation that is incompatible with action and even with the will to action, the very thought of action."

Inward and outward—that is the natural rhythm of life; good because it is natural; good because it works. All human beings, without exception, need both. The proportions may be different for the monk and the physicist, the guru and the shoemaker, but we all share the need. That is why there is nothing contradictory in the fact that in an era of turning inward we are also stressing expanded human relationship and concern with injustice.

In fact, just as the noblest people in the past combined both ways, so do the noblest people in the present. For example, it is morning at the Institute in Arizona. Sister Mary Grace has just come back from an hour's contemplation by herself in the chapel. Now she is planting flowers from the desert by the guest house we share. She will be here only a few weeks, but she wants to leave something living and growing behind her. What a gentle, unworldly person she is, one thinks, her life devoted to contemplation and solitude! You think so—until you look a little further and discover that in New Orleans,

where she lives the rest of the year, she successfully runs
an organization for the rehabilitation of tough young
male ex-convicts.

I think of others whose life exemplifies this maturing
rhythm. No one was more compassionate or cared more
about serving his fellow men than the late Rabbi Abraham Joshua Heschel. He marched with his fellow clergymen in Alabama in 1965 and struggled for years, at great
cost, against the war in Vietnam. Yet he was a mystic
whose many books are as spiritual as they are practical.
I interviewed him once in his cluttered dark little office—
a white-bearded scholar, smoking a long, long cigar. The
conversation was too warm, too instantaneous for a tape
recorder; but I would give a great deal to have a record of
it, for it was spiritually moving, yet witty: a prayer and a
program of action. Marching in the civil-rights protests
of the sixties, Heschel once said, "I feel as if my legs were
praying." And yet he beautifully wrote elsewhere, "Man's
walled mind has no access to a ladder upon which he can,
on his own strength, rise to the knowledge of God. Yet
his soul is endowed with translucent windows that open
to the beyond." For him surely there was no duality
between serving God in action and in prayer.

Once, too, on a plane in the early years of the civil-
rights crusade, I found, to my delight, that the seat mate
who, like myself, was surrounded by books and papers
was Martin Luther King, Jr. We were both writing
speeches that called for explosive action. Nevertheless,
in that unforgettable two-hour conversation what we
talked about was not civil rights but theology—what we
believed about man and God, what we thought about sin
and forgiveness, what it meant to grow, why solitude
mattered.

Several years ago I also had a long and unforgettable interview with Abraham Maslow. He was already ailing from the heart condition which was to cause his death so soon thereafter, and he had promised me only a few minutes, but in the end we talked for hours. Though he lay on a couch part of the time, the memory which stays with me most is of his own urgent vitality as he emphasized again and again that it is the healthy, vigorous person experiencing his life, growing, contributing, to whom peak experience comes naturally and often.

Are we really less likely to find fulfillment in our lives because we are using all of our capacities, inner as well as outer? Must we stop loving and serving our fellow men because we are ourselves growing spiritually? I once asked this question of a Congregational minister renowned both for his spirituality and for his activism. He answered indignantly, "Why can't I have a prayer meeting, a charismatic gathering, on a Wednesday night and still get my parishioners together on Saturday to help me support housing for the poor?" Why not indeed?

The rhythm of action and inwardness is as necessary as the rhythm of day and night; and it was never more needed than it is now, if only because we are a city people and will never again become a rural populace—a city people living with a daily congeries of suffering, struggling, frustrating, human beings, building a civilization, not a hermitage.

John Peer Nugent, who wrote so earnestly of our need for each other, pleads also for the appreciation of the city. The city, he says, "is where Early Man stopped running long enough to consider more than personal survival. It is where he thought enough to write and paint and leave some permanent artifacts which future societies could build and are still building. Maybe nomads thought good things as they moved about under the stars. We'll never know, because they didn't create the tools for recording. Those tools came when the settlement concept dawned; so did something called civilization. Great books and stimulating ideas have come from the cities. . . . It is from the city's soul that Horace and Euripides drew inspiration and stimulation. The city yields food for growth, the protein of life, the pulse of presence. . . . The city is at once the very pulse of life, and the face of death— two things we all have to confront daily. The city is a high-rise fire, a marketplace of faces, a museum; it is the sight of a black man walking with a white woman, the soulful sound of a clarinet coming from an open window over a whirling laundromat; the worry that someone in a tenement is shooting up or ripping off any plumbing with copper content; it is the hope that from a university complex will come a cure for cancer. . . . It is where one faces up not to self so much as to duty. The city is where man . . . decides to act, not weigh the alternatives to acting."

Summing up, the more we are inward, the more we are truly human; and the more human we are the more we can and should care for and serve our fellows. We turn to others; we turn inward to ourselves—in a cycle as natural as the winter sleeping of the seed in order that when the springtime comes it may bloom. We build ourselves; then offer ourselves; then build again.

The problem is to discover a *way* to put them together; to find structures in which their harmonious interplay can serve us best. To do this we shall have to start that teaching early in life, and we shall have to set up institutional supports, models to which all of us can look for help. Right now, we nowhere really teach this rhythm. Children do not learn it at school or at home. They are not taught to go first to the deep Self and learn and grow and then give away what they have found like a grace to the world, and we'll have to find out how to teach that.

Fortunately, models are proliferating rapidly. For example, some of the best energies of young Quakers at the present time are directed toward creating communes or life centers where, in a life style of simplicity, they can recover at one and the same time true community, a direction for service, and perhaps also mystic consciousness.

Here and there, also, a city church provides a place to see this rhythm in action. The Church of the Savior in Washington, D.C., is a perfect example. This small church—its membership is little more than one hundred, though an additional three to four hundred work with the church in various ways—has accomplished prodigious things. There are stiff requirements for entering it, even an interning process; and universal tithing of time and money is insisted on as a bare minimum. This year's budget is about $250,000. They run the Potter's House, a coffee shop in the inner city; they maintain a retreat farm; they work among alcoholics, the mentally ill, abandoned children; and they have housing projects. Each evening there is a supper for old people, priced at about twenty-five cents. The tithing of time as well as money means that each group in the church has a task to do; but each group also has an inward task. For example, a group of young people who lived by choice in a poverty-stricken area, tutoring children, helping solve manifold problems, nonetheless set aside an hour and a half each day for individual meditation. The numerous mission groups—perhaps they could be called task forces—practice meditation with the same seriousness they give to the tasks of their hands. Elizabeth O'Connor, who has chronicled the life of this church in several books, says of these mission groups that they are "structures to hold the inward and the outward."

We need institutional change if we are to redirect the life of our times into a fruitful rhythm; but we also need change in our personal lives. What must be learned is the habit of seeing ourselves as total human beings, imagining ourselves as people who need to grow as much as we need to act. We must accept responsibility for finding a way to go inward, and then a way to unite our learning with our action; for there is no way to heaven without each other, and it is unbearable to gain inward wisdom and be unable to use it. After peak experiences, Dr. Maslow told me, generous and loving people often ask for help. "What should I do with it?" they plead.

Perhaps, indeed, the measure of the authenticity of our inward journey is the degree to which it teaches us to battle the structures of injustice and oppression. Indeed, one of the greatest contributions the meditator can make to a troubled world is the political one. He is, for one thing, well qualified to teach a simpler way of life as against a too materialistic one; a doing without in order to share with a starving, dying world; and he has much to contribute to that profound understanding of other people which should lie at the roots of both domestic and foreign policy. Thomas Merton, says his biographer, "was a hermit-monk who loved the world and was deeply moved by its suffering and injustice." He rarely left the monastery, yet in the very beginning wrote passionately about war and the nuclear-arms race and racism. And, indeed, such contemporary forms of meditation can be—and often are—profoundly political.

Technology too is itself no curse, but rather a blessing which must be wholeheartedly accepted as a wonderful partner for achieving a better world. The flaw is not in its existence but in our failure to partner it with a greater priority—the building of a humane and human world.

What shall we do about the diminishing resources of our planet? How shall we prevent war, an unthinkable holocaust in an atomic age? How shall we be rid of political corruption? We *can't* think our way through. Perhaps we can intuit our way by a deeper understanding of ourselves and other people. How many "practical" politicians we would exchange for one statesman—one man of wisdom and vision!

It is good that we are witnessing a rebirth of the monastic, utopian tradition, writes Harvey Cox. "A society needs seedplots and models. It needs a variety of experimental tryouts of new institutions, life patterns, values, symbols, and rituals."

They have found the way to live—these mystic-activists of past and present; and they are the best hope that the cult of inwardness will last, the best hope that the meaning and significance of this change can be understood. *Time* magazine ended an article on the new inward movement with a statement of the utmost significance. "The problem for Americans and others caught up in the West's renewed search for the sacred," said *Time*'s commentator, "will be just how and where to strike a fruitful balance between reason and imagination, between discipline and intuition, between a creative awe of the worlds man can only contemplate and a creative concern for the world he lives in."

CHAPTER 8

The Tree of Tomorrow

〰〰〰〰〰〰〰〰〰〰〰〰〰〰〰〰〰〰〰〰〰

I am ending this book on a spring day in a country inn in the Litchfield hills of Connecticut. The days are shadowy; the warmth of the earth has not yet declared itself; the trees are budded, but they are still only a promise.

Much joy has befallen me in the course of this book; and a great grief has come as well. I am now alone in my life in the special way of the widowed. I sit here looking into the sanctuary of that life, the deep self which, like a well, spirals down toward the roots of the world, knowing that I am looking not for the answers to problems but for the linkages of memory, of time past, time present, time future, and for that place where each of us, fragile and alone, feels the bond with other people and with God.

I am alone now in a special way; but each of us in a true sense is alone in the world. Every man, every woman, is Ulysses on a journey to invent the world, find the world; and each of us is a Robinson Crusoe on an island in eternal time, a Robinson Crusoe who, in the last essence, finds in his own interior his final sustenance and who forages alone for his survival, his courage, his enlightenment.

In the period of gestation that follows on grief one discovers, indeed, that everything of importance happens first in the deep Self. Here sorrow does its cleansing work; here memory lodges; here the new growing painfully begins. It is not hard to see that here, too, lies the future of the individual, and so of the race. Forced, of necessity, to the deep Self to find one's balance again, one can almost sense the seed sprouting. Indeed, we carry the seeds for growing within ourselves as we carry our genes; and perhaps it is true, too, that we carry the long-distance seeds, the latencies of evolution.

At any rate, with the cumulative language of the book fresh in my thoughts, I look now not only for my own tree of tomorrow, but for the one we all share. What is it that is growing here? What future will follow the unexpected inward revolution which has already begun to change our lives?

Forecasting the future is often like shooting an arrow at the stars; but in the year 1975, one thing, I think, can be said with certainty: we are *ripe for change*. A unique combination of circumstances has made the moment right for the voyager into inner space. What we are witnessing is a time of mind-blowing crisis, despair and rocketlike change —change we can't halt. But this change and despair coincide with an explosion of knowledge and an awareness of alternatives such as man has never experienced before. Combined, they form one of those historic moments in human existence when the human creature can leap like a spark in the wind from present to future.

Our technological industrial world has fumbled and blundered its way like a great blinded giant, powerful and intelligent, lacking only the eyes to see where it was going.

Thinking of it so, playwright William Gibson, whose book *A Season in Heaven* was written after a summer spent in Spain with a group of young people at a Transcendental Meditation seminar, concluded the book with an ironic account of his flight home. The stewardess, he says,

> came down the aisle with copies of the *New York Times.*
> . . . In Washington a senator had been shot and robbed in his driveway; in Northern Ireland five more were dead of Christian differences. In Indo-China the planes the senator had sponsored were seeding the villages with bombs, bombs, bombs . . . and so on, page after page, the people of the day running around like decapitated chickens; and when I turned to the arts, half the ads were of pornographic movies. I was back in the real world. Sure was great to get away from them crazy kids.

Perhaps we had to come to this knowledge of need, to our new clarity of vision, by the shattering route we have taken; perhaps we had to face the worst in ourselves before we could begin to think about how to transcend it. Perhaps a volcano had to blow in order to lift the low ceiling of our pragmatic age, and to set whirling the winds of change.

At any rate, most of us know that we can no longer afford to remain as we are. A sense of telescoped time, a change and an unpredictability, hangs over our world, and we are in a race to use this change rather than to be used by it.

We are ripe for change because we need it; but we are ripe for it also because suddenly *we can have it.* For the first time we know *how* to change human consciousness, how to "raise the process of awareness." After years of research, years in which her own wonder was constantly fed by what was happening in her laboratory, Barbara Brown exclaimed, "Only in this decade have the parallel evolutions of man's technology and of his mind created the kind of environment that allows a better understanding of the magnitude, the order, and the power of inner space."

What can happen in such an open situation? The possibilities seem almost infinite. Some of the prospects, indeed, read like science fiction. For example, what about conveying important military information in wartime through telepathy—that from-the-depths-of-one-to-the-depths-of-the-other communication which the Russians have been laboring to set up? What about keeping alive in the desert without water by a mind control of one's urinary output? What about a conscious "thinking with energy"? An elimination of pain except as a warning signal?

Other possibilities are perhaps less utilitarian and more profound, going to the roots of the perfectibility of the human being and the life of the nation. In this area experts surveying the scene promise "a larger experience of the dimensions of reality"; "a lifetime—not just a school time—of learning"; "another stage of human life beyond *homo labore,* even beyond the public-spirited man"; "the extension of the limits of human ability"; "a new way of relating to other people"; a new way of "creating a loving society in which community rather than individualism is typical."

Specifically, here are some of the possibilities which may be part of everyday life for the men and women of tomorrow:

First, we will almost certainly find ourselves in the future taking meditation and other altered states of consciousness seriously; taking for granted a goal of steadily increasing awareness for all of us; paying more attention to intuition, dreams, imagery. We'll set aside *time for meditation,* in a more planned way than we are doing now. Rest houses, retreat houses, may be available in every community where people can be guaranteed absolute silence and privacy when they need it. Perhaps we will learn to do as many Easterners do—take a time out of our lives for solitary growing. In some Oriental countries boys, as a part of growing up, are sent to monasteries to serve as monks for a given period. Variations of that are possible in Western countries: retreat houses where anyone can go for a week, a month, a year of solitude; local places of meditation in towns and cities available for any hour of the day.

A dream takes shape in my own mind—a dream that someday such places of retreat will be in reach of everyone, offering training times in the lives of young men and women, refreshing times in middle age, growing times in old age when the job is over. In these checkout places, you'd be able to be silent and alone if that was what you wanted. But there would be areas of discovery too where one could study how to go down to the deep self for wisdom and growing, or where one could learn from noble people about the victories and failures of human beings and about the nature of life and love. And there would be other areas too where there were spacious walls of books and the sound of music or of waterfalls or of wind in the trees. Here human beings could grow and learn and rest, and from here return to help build a better world. Here being in touch with ourselves would help us to be in touch with others.

Perhaps we might even set aside special communities of people whose forte is to teach the meditative arts to students of politics and economics, or to be themselves a gathered community where alternatives of all kinds are submitted to the meditative consciousness.

Such retreats are still a dream; but lesser ones are growing everywhere and will almost certainly continue to do so; and they are a taken-for-granted part of life for many of today's young people. This generation of American young people have, in fact, discovered their own ways. They go to conferences and seminars lasting a day, a week, a month, where the focus of attention is the inward self; they form communes and live for several months or several years in quiet places untouched by modern industrial life, and observe periods set apart for formal meditation; or they travel to the East and live in ashrams; they choose hermitages and live alone; or they just simplify their lives in the city so that they have time for inwardness.

The moment is right, too, for change in the *schools*. Today as never before we need a curriculum, a style of educational life, which prepares the child for something more than adjustment to a technological society—prepares him instead to help build a new compassionate world, and permits him to bring to that world all the gifts he has.

School change has been in the air for decades, and the consciences of educators have long been bruised by the terrifying truism that none of us uses more than 5 to 10 percent of his intellectual capacities, and that children, creative as seeds when they are small, have lost most of their joyful response to the world even before they reach adolescence. So the educational scene has been a kaleidoscope of designs for change, but in fact little has happened. It is scarcely too much to say that our schools have basically changed very little since I was a child.

They may change, however, under the influence of the

enormous discoveries made by the inward revolution. We now *know* how we have underrated the capacities of all of us; we know what a meager part of our consciousness we have been using. As the leaders of the new movement grow more and more articulate, it will be increasingly difficult to toss aside their findings; and, in fact, experiments prompted by the new consciousness movement are popping up everywhere. Ananda Marga, for example, has recently opened five schools in different parts of the country; and they hope to take the child "from sensory experience to the actual realization of higher consciousness."

Emerging from their laboratory, Masters and Houston are working in schools in Seattle, New York, Connecticut, to teach children to use as many of their potentials as possible. They are particularly anxious to teach them to think with images—an ability we've been leaching away from our children for years by our concentration on verbal learning.

We have done so little to balance our concentration on words, that even Masters and Houston, indefatigable researchers though they are, are able to think of only one fairly large-scale effort to preserve the imaging capacity of children. This experiment, Dr. Houston says, was conducted by the Jaensch brothers in special schools in Germany in the 1920s, and, she says, it found that children "taught to use the image-thought process were, by the time they reached their teens, more creative; they retained the capacity to draw, and scored higher on intelligence tests than comparable children whose imagery was inhibited by educational processes too oriented to the verbal."

In their own school experiments, Masters and Houston have found ample confirmation of this. The child who can interpret his world in images—often symbolic images

—as well as in words is more creative and more efficient, more aware of the riches of his body and mind; and—Masters and Houston believe—if we begin such training in childhood, the acceleration of thinking that the human race needs so much right now may well be acquired "without trance, drugs, or other marked alterations of consciousness."

Perhaps the child of the future will see colors we scarcely imagine, will experience the world around him as sharply, most of the time, as he now does only when the circus comes to town. He will, at any rate, almost certainly be accustomed to a far more profound use of human consciousness, a far wider awareness of the totality of self.

The child of the future will also learn to take for granted, in ways we do not, the magic kinship of mind and body. Dr. Joe Kamija, experimenting at San Francisco's Langley Porter Neuropsychiatric Institution, thinks we will have a new kind of sensitivity training "in which children would become aware of the goings-on inside their bodies and their minds and, eventually, learn to control them." Just as children are sometimes blindfolded and asked to name the objects they touch in order to give them experience in sensing the outside world, so they might be attached to feedback machines to learn about their inside world. Such machines may also be used in conjunction with teaching machines, suggests Barbara Brown, "to let the child know when his attention is wandering. That way children could acquire mental and physical disciplines more quickly than they normally would."

Still other teachers offer models and seedplots for whole school systems, radically changed from those of the past; and it is no coincidence that the people who come up with these models are often those whose original interest in educational change led rather swiftly to an equal interest in the expanding consciousness. One thinks, for example, of the model school George Leonard proposes in his book *Education and Ecstasy*. He sees a grassy play field encircled with flowers. "Gleaming geodesic domes and translucent, tentlike structures are scattered randomly among graceful trees"; children move about from one learning environment to another; have impassioned encounters under the trees with teachers; daydream. The school is open from eight in the morning to six in the afternoon, and the children come and go and do not stay all day.

In one of the great domes of this school there are learning consoles, and computers with an individual screen for each child; and children and computer together pour imaginative learning displays onto the screens. There is a "Quiet Dome" for silence and meditation. There are places where children can make their own devices for learning. Another project re-creates life in other eras, other times; and there are Water and Body domes where the children exercise, swim, and get acquainted with the resources of their bodies.

In other areas, children practice control of respiration and pulse rate. They may play games which bring together math and logic with music and the sense of touch. There are a play field, a room where visiting parents may be fed, a library. There are discovery tents where teachers set up educational environments. Here a bulletin board outside tells what is happening in the tent, and sometimes so many children want to explore it that the bulletin board has to flash "Come back later" signals.

There are groups in which values are discussed, in which the children may weep over the wars of history—wars they no longer experience—or struggle to say what they believe about issues of right and wrong.

One thing is sure. If we cannot do at least some of these moving things it will not be because of the children; they will not be the ones for whom such change will be hard. People experimenting with new innovations in the schools have found the children fascinated and absorbed. I know; for a few years, when our children were small and we needed money badly, I substituted in the high schools and junior highs in my city—surely one of the most onerous jobs on earth, comparable only to hunting lions with a broom or motorcycling on a wire across the Grand Canyon. But it did bring me—instructively—into contact with scores of teachers, and with the classes which were marked by their teaching for good and for bad; and I still remember—cringing as I did then—the advice that came one day from an elderly teacher who surveyed with disapproval the enthusiastic but argumentative free-style classroom in which I was happily trying to keep afloat.

"You mustn't go over their heads," she said. "You're trying to get too much out of them, and that's why they're noisy and excited. They're pretty limited, you know, and it's best to keep things simple."

I was intimidated; nevertheless, I went out the door rebelling silently, oppressed by a vision of each child in a cage through the interstices of which I must insert small neat packages of learning. The truth was that I had found it otherwise. I had found that in the presence of new ideas, new pictures of the future, new understanding about the nature of life, young people not only could "go over their heads" but longed to.

After all, many children greet learning with total delight; and many experiments show how we underrate children's ability to learn and their joy in learning. We repeat calmly the much bandied-about comment that children, hugely creative at five and six, have lost most of their creativity before adolescence; we repeat it calmly as though it were not a monstrous thing. Yet anyone who has had any experience with gifted children knows how they love to learn. I remember a child who stayed after school for hours to find out how to write a play, and another who constructed an African environment from her geography "just for fun"; my own grandson made a computer at the age of eleven. Less gifted children are not as individually resourceful, but when the project links with something they care about they too "love to learn."

We must consciously start multiplying ways to enlarge the consciousness of children. We shall need in the future all kinds of models. It is likely that we'll be experimenting with a wide range of ideas for enlarging consciousness and increasing creativity; and that one of these ideas will be meditation, since it so swiftly and certainly takes us to the creating center of ourselves.

Schools will change—how much we have yet to discover —and, as we suggested in an earlier chapter, so will *churches.* For one thing, they will be affected by the upsurge of religious longing outside their walls, and by the unavoidable awareness of what this longing has to say about people's most profound needs.

They must especially be affected by the religious longings of the young; for if these are inchoate, undisciplined, nontheological, they are nonetheless passionately real. A host of commentators agree that there is more religious interest among young people today than at any other time in the century. I think of a young man I met recently in the diner of a train who said, "I am passionately interested in religion because I have none." We began to speak of religious consciousness at the table. When we returned to our seats in a crowded car where it was impossible to sit together, he crouched on the floor beside my seat for an hour, and, as the train jerked and rattled exhaustingly on its way, we talked about nothing less than the nature of God.

I think, too, of a time some years ago when I was speaking at the evening meeting of a church group which included both old and young people. In the question period afterward, I asked the older people what they thought youth wanted of the church. The answers—we were then in the era of the secular city—ranged from "a place for social life" to "a place to meet their friends," "a guide to conduct" and "a place where they can help others." Then someone in the audience turned it back to me. "What do you think?" she said.

I can claim in my answer no clairvoyant wisdom. I had just finished doing a survey for *Redbook* of the opinions of young Protestant adults on various religious questions, and I remembered how often they had written a single answer to a question on the purpose of religion. I responded with that answer. "They want to find the meaning of life," I said. It seemed an unremarkable and rather obvious comment, but I have never forgotten the reaction. All over the church young people spontaneously burst into clapping, some even jumping from their seats.

Right now, this is even more the "condition that prevails." Everywhere young people are full of spiritual longing. Because that longing expresses itself so frequently in bizarre ways, it is as often written off by sophisticated churchmen. But it is huge, and, unless fiercely discouraged, it will not go away; and the pressure of that longing bombards the doors of the churches.

Some churchmen cannot bring themselves to call it a religious revival as long as the young people, while beating on the walls, still refuse to come in and indeed often "follow after strange gods"—the gods of the very faiths to which the church has long been sending missionaries. But perhaps there is too much concern about the fact that the most popular and mystical movements are outside the established church. Historically, it has usually been so. One thinks of the Quakers; of the rise of Zen in the sixth century; indeed, of the coming of Christianity itself. And it frequently happens that visionary experience and concentration on the inner life are the hallmark of these movements, which often come just in time to fertilize and revive religious institutions that have become too oriented to the establishments of their time.

Nevertheless, a growing number of reporters note a new stirring in the churches as well. *U.S. News & World Report* quotes Dr. John W. Meister, director of the Council of Theological Seminaries for the United Presbyterian Church in the U.S.A. "There's no doubt," he says, "we're going to have a spiritual revival, and I think the establishment churches will have a big part in it. In the social excitement of the last ten years, religion has been sort of beside the point; but now things have changed. I have yet to see a church that isn't experiencing a new vitality of some sort."

The key ingredient in the religious revival, according to this report, is "a renewed interest in the more personal and emotional aspects of religion and a greater emphasis on the needs of the individual person." A renewed interest, too, in the merging concern for social change and religious experiment with a traditional and transcendent faith.

One step in the right direction would be a willingness to try out new formats in the church. After all, it is the gospel the church teaches which is unchangeable, not the forms in which it is expressed. Perhaps—since the changing of format in any institution is always so difficult—we might begin with small steps. We might, for example, set up one experimental church in each large community and let its members try out various styles of worship and service.

What, I wonder, would the churches be like if each individual could design his own? The late Thomas Sugrue, an ecumenical Catholic who would have been at home with much that is happening in the new movement, once wrote unforgettably about a church for tomorrow which he had constructed in imagination while he was still a boy.

"It was very large," he wrote, "with great skylights and enormous windows so that all day it was flooded with sunshine. From its sides two buildings extend as wings; they also had skylights and great windows. One of them was a library, the other contained a series of rooms where people went to consult with priests and priestesses about the nature of God and the destiny of man." In the rear of the building there was a huge greenhouse full of fountains, flowers and singing birds.

The priests and priestesses lived in the building. Here they studied, meditated and talked among themselves, and a flow of the world's knowledge came to them constantly. They also "ministered to the ill and to the afflicted, and consulted with anyone who came to ask questions of truth or to seek counsel and guidance." If a priest and priestess wished to marry, they were given the blessing of the church and "sent into the world as servants of the poor, the helpless and uninstructed."

They went, all of them, wherever they were needed.

If a woman of the town fell ill a priestess went to nurse her. If a man of the town was arrested, a priest went to represent him in court. Those who were drunken or homeless or afraid came to the church and were succored. Its doors were never shut, its lights were never dimmed. . . . Any man could enter the church and ask for a priest or a priestess and speak with him or with her of the things that troubled him.

On Sunday a priest or a priestess celebrated Mass. . . . Those who wished to receive communion did so, but not at this Mass. Each communicant passed the night somewhere in the church, praying, meditating, reading. An hour before dawn those who felt ready gathered at the altar and knelt before it. As the sun rose a priest who had also spent the night in preparation came and celebrated Mass, giving communion to those who awaited him.

What is important is not that this special vision be accepted. What matters is that the most imaginative minds be set to work to find through the new inward movement such creative ways of changing the church, not in its faith but in its format.

The church will change. So will other things in the world of tomorrow as the explosion of ideas seeds the community with new life. For one thing, we will see psychology exploring even further in the world of the frankly spiritual. Dr. Dean told the American Psychiatric Association that metapsychiatry will be part of the curriculum of scientists tomorrow if not today; and the encyclopedia *Man, Myth, and Magic,* commenting on the degree to which scientists and doctors are researching the untapped powers of the mind—including the faculty of extrasensory perception, the possibilities of mind over matter, the worldwide reports of psychic and paranormal occurrences —says that "already the evidence is building up which could establish 'supernatural manifestations' as capacities natural to man."

Earlier I referred to "Transpersonal Psychology"—a movement that is growing rapidly and is sometimes called "a fourth force in psychology." Transpersonal therapists, writes Sam Keen in *Psychology Today,*

> may introduce their clients to meditation or mantras, or help them create a spiritual discipline from yoga, or other religious traditions. But their main innovation is in a new definition of the world preview, the perspective within which therapy must be conducted. Both therapist and client are committed to the realization of the human vocation as a self-conscious participant in a divine order. The only way out of alienation is the vision of the transcendent citizenship of the human spirit.

Prevention and cure of disease through inward disciplines will continue to bring some of the most startling changes. The new understanding of the relationship of mind and body—an understanding to which meditation has contributed so much—will make huge changes in the therapies that are available both for the diseases we've been calling physical and for those we've labeled mental. We may learn to think of disease as mind-body dysfunction, and of health as mind-body harmony, and we may use yoga as medicine. But in any case what we'll be learning is not more about sickness but more about health.

As a result, life will be considerably changed for all of us. People practicing therapeutic relaxation may live longer and more productively. The intelligent use of our inner selves will help us recover more effectively from illness—even organic illness. To some extent we will be able to tell the body what we need and let it heal itself. Specifically, we will be well equipped to handle such things as stress and insomnia, to lower blood pressure, to change or regulate heart rate, to relieve headache through muscle and blood-vessel control, and to become aware of disturbances that, if left unchecked, can lead to illnesses.

"In five years," Barbara Brown predicted correctly in 1971, "there will be biofeedback centers all over the country, in which people can learn all manner of mind and body functions." And the most way-out among the prophets suggests that this and other mind-over-body techniques may be used to cut off the flow of blood to a tumor and thus starve it, to regulate glandular secretions and even to control the activity of a single cell. Maybe if you were lost in the desert without water you could control your kidneys and slow the rate at which they remove water from your blood, thus stretching your water supply. Perhaps if you were getting ready for an exam or a hard-fought case in court, or a speech, you might be able to slow your heart and lower your blood pressure, thus reducing anxiety. Perhaps if you were hurt on a camping trip, far from a doctor, and bleeding dangerously, you might be able to stop the blood flow with the power of your mind.

Andrew Weil sums it up. "I believe," he writes, "that an intellectual revolution is in progress in America; and that it will ultimately change things like medicine and psychology beyond recognition." The essence of this change is a growing awareness of and acceptance of the force of the nonrational, which pervades the human mind and the external universe; it will transform many of our lifeless intellectual institutions.

One aspect of that intellectual revolution will be a great openness—a willingness to question everything which we have hitherto thought of as unchangeable reality. Prodded by our ability to reach inward to our authentic selves, we will be trying many alternative styles of life, many ways of being human. Communal forms may be less and less confined to the young. It may be more common for several families to try living together; so, too, may the old in communes of their own design; and so may many people who share an objective, like the Quaker communes.

Political and economic life will be affected as we learn to use the meditative arts to understand ourselves and, by extension, each other. "This is the fullest development of meditation," writes John White. "Personal evolution becomes social revolution. By changing yourself, you help to change the world."

After years of being awash in cries of "Relevance, relevance," we are experiencing a revulsion from the word. But, in fact, there is nothing wrong with being relevant. What is wrong is in failing to understand the profound and subtle meanings of this useful word. To be relevant is not necessarily to follow the customs and views of our time, but to see with sensitivity where we are so that our remedies can avail. In that light the most "relevant" thing we can say politically is that the ability to increase human capacity, once a dream for mankind, has now become a cry for self-preservation.

Social concern itself, in fact, has taken new directions

under the combined impetus of the inward revolution and the social fervor of the sixties. It has grown less exuberant, more thoughtful, more widespread and, amongst a small instructed minority, more sophisticated. There seems to be a growing understanding of human need, human grief, human injustices, and of the mechanisms for assuaging them; a more sober, less idealistic, less judgmental view of the depth of problems; an awareness of their seriousness and their comparative difficulty of solution.

Since a whole lifetime will not be enough to exhaust the new knowledge of what our minds can do, learning will be accepted as a lifetime pursuit. Already we have gone quite a way in that direction with the establishment of adult education and the appearance of seventy-five-year-old candidates for university degrees. But with the understanding of the meaning of higher consciousness and with the increased capacity to reach it, we will understand lifetime education in new and much richer ways. Problems, of course, will not go away in individual lives, or in the nation; but there will be a potent minority effort to approach them at deeper levels of understanding.

We will learn new ways of being closer to each other, even of teaching strangers to be closer to each other. People may choose to give up success and achievements which meant a great deal to the citizens of yesterday; male and female stereotypes will continue to change, but the change will go in the direction of women's liberation only as long as that movement can demonstrate a concern for a truly humane way of life.

We may find ourselves communicating with each other in a warmer, more sensitive, more instantaneous way. Communal, meditative and encounter groups have already discovered the warmth and understanding of being together at another level of consciousness. Perhaps what is really happening is that our ideas of what people should mean to each other are changing. We want to be at once honest and loving, compassionate and humble. In fact, with many people the very word "love" has changed, broadened, grown less sentimental, more honest, and is often directed to the stranger who, in our mobile world, will vanish so soon.

Change itself will continue at a great speed or perhaps, more accurately, will be resumed when the present nostalgic period has passed. We will accept—we are already accepting—a kind of Protean existence in which there is change not only around us but within us—in which we change to match the changing world.

We will in one way or another give more thought to the value systems of our society. Concern with big ideas like human destiny and evolutionary change will preoccupy many people, who will not find a need to apologize for talking about soul and spirit. All kinds of people will be helping to answer the most important question of all—"What do we want from the future?"

Tomorrow's man "will be a visionary," says Jean Houston; "he will have access to his unconscious and its creative and other processes. He will have access to his imageries, to think with, create with, and to be entertained by, . . . [to] an imagination so rich that in the past it has usually been experienced only by the exceptional creative artist."

In fact, not only children but adults as well will become accustomed to a far more profound use of human consciousness. Certainly men and women of the future will regard joy and ecstasy as part of their birthright. There will be more emphasis on trusting the intuition, the emotions and, above all, the *insights* of the innermost self. The rejection of technocracy which characterized the early development of the counterculture will give way to a greater willingness to see that there is beneficence in a properly controlled technocracy; but the emphasis on the importance of the individual and on the value of those ways of arriving at truth which are beyond the technocracy will continue.

But the most important result of the revolution in consciousness may be a new sense of the *dignity of man*—a dignity which has been dealt so many blows through the centuries of Copernicus and Darwin and Freud. Persistently, steadily, through all the long painful centuries, men have struggled to believe that they were more than dust; and in this era the belief has found its way into the laboratory and into other unexpected areas. How meekly in the last decades we accepted the loss of this human stature! But it is returning, for the more man's mind can direct his destiny, the more dignity he has; and the more he feels that his personal identity reflects a power encompassing the universe, the more that dignity grows.

These are startling, evolving possibilities, a dazzling vision of a world "based on a more noble notion of the human mind and its gifts." It is a dazzling vision, but a frightening one as well. Exhilarating to many people, it is overwhelming to others. And there is reason for fear; for what is at stake is nothing less than learning how to handle a swift, evolutionary change in that most individual and hitherto sacred area of our lives—our inmost selves. Inner space is full of perils, full of hidden pits and snares, and nothing could be more dangerous than a blind acceptance of everything that is offered.

The trouble is that psychic gifts—like all other gifts—are morally neutral, and a psychic experience can be a long way from spiritual growing. To use the mind's marvelous capacities simply to startle is like using a wonderful memory simply in order to awe people with, say, the lists of numbers you can remember. "Signs and wonders" for their own sake are useful only as signals that something is there. Divorced from spiritual growth, they have little significance for mankind. That is why the Eastern guru makes so little of his really astonishing powers; perhaps that is why Jesus so easily dismissed his miracles. He had not come, he seemed to say, in order to walk on the water or heal the sick, but in order to change men's hearts. And certainly that is why mere performers of psychic parlor tricks may be regarded with curiosity and interest but seldom with the homage reserved for saints and mystics. The humbling fact is that to move safely in the world of the psychic one needs to be a good person.

We must not minimize the perils, and neither must we forget the questions which remain unanswered. For example: Who leads? Who follows? Whose vision do we trust? To some extent now the young are leading us. In a very real way it is the children's crusade. That's fine; but to idolize them, to feel they can do no wrong, is a disservice to them as well as to us. The mistakes of their immaturity are all around us, and we must move up to help them.

In summary, we are brought up against ultimate questions; we can make catastrophic errors; we urgently need wisdom. But the fire has been found, the power is now irreversibly here, and the answer to the problems is not to turn back the clock but to find our way into the future.

From that viewpoint meditation is not an escape from

daily living but a preparation for it, and what is of surpassing importance is what we bring back from the experience. Like pearl divers, meditators plunge deep into the inner ocean of consciousness and hope to come swimming back to the surface with jewels of great price. The treasures are important; but so is the journey itself. If it does nothing else, the inward journey teaches us the complexity of the human mind—the many layers in which it operates, the depths and heights it can reach, the possibilities barely glimpsed.

Once there was a human creature who emerged triumphantly from the thralldom of walking on all fours, came out of the trees, discovered the cave, the family, the fire for cooking. History moved on, and there were other human beings who discovered the garden, the soil to be worked, the food to be grown at will. Somewhere at some time evolving humans encountered the mythic tree in the Garden of Eden, the soul-making knowledge of good and evil, the demand to be moral. Later the door opened to the physical world, the geographic world; continents were crossed, islands found, harbors opened to venturing ships, minerals discovered in the heart of the earth; and eventually there was the passage of the skies, the exploration of space.

And now we are on the last, most dangerous and most glorious of them all, the discovery of the wonders of inner space; the answer to "Who am I?" the pilgrimage to the hidden mystery of human nature and of its relationship to the gods. Once more the long line of historic man—who has been snatching the Promethean fire not once but many times—now has another blazing brand to seize.

The new insights could transform our lives and the lives of our nation almost beyond recognition. Perhaps now we can begin to think of ourselves not only as people of action but as contemplatives too: people who want to know and understand themselves as much as they want to act, people who are able to look within to find there wisdom and courage and understanding—sometimes even love—to match the terrifying world outside.

But even if this new movement is only a passing phenomenon, it cannot fail to leave its impress behind as a part of the pattern out of which the future comes. "As numerous persons individually enlarge the dimensions of their experience," writes Progoff, "a special atmosphere of reality comes into the world."

In any case, the wisdom of Socrates still rings from the past. If we try to find out what is unknown, he said, "we shall be better and braver . . . than if we believe that what we do not know is impossible to find out and that we need not even try."